CARL H. MILAM

and

The United Nations Library

Edited and

with an Introduction

by

DORIS CRUGER DALE

The Scarecrow Press, Inc.

Metuchen, N.J.   1976

Library of Congress Cataloging in Publication Data

Milam, Carl Hastings, 1884-1963.
    Carl H. Milam and the United Nations Library.

    Bibliography: p.
    Includes index.
    1. Milam, Carl Hastings, 1884-1963. 2. United
Nations, Dag Hammarskjöld Library. I. Dale, Doris
Cruger. II. Title.
Z720. M62A32   1976   020'. 92'4   76-14866
ISBN 0-8108-0941-9

Dedicated to the
memory of my father

CONTENTS

ACKNOWLEDGMENTS

Appreciation and gratitude are extended to Carl Milam's daughter, Mrs. William A. Seidler, Jr., who very kindly lent the author the diary her father kept while he was librarian of the United Nations and gave permission for its publication. Thanks are also extended to the University of Chicago Press, publishers of The Library Quarterly, and to the American Library Association, publishers of the (former) ALA Bulletin, for permission to reprint from their journals the two articles by Milam and Lydenberg respectively.

Mary M. Shaw graciously gave her permission for the publication of portions of her husband's report on the United Nations Library. Both Luther H. Evans and Arthur C. Breycha-Vauthier consented to having the report they co-authored with Carl Milam and Ralph Beals published in this volume.

The faculty members of Morris Library, Southern Illinois University at Carbondale, have been very helpful in the author's research. The author's office staff in Carbondale typed the manuscript.

The author would especially like to thank her husband for his encouragement and advice. Without his cheerful sharing of household chores, this book could not have been finished.

Introduction:

THE INTERNATIONAL LIBRARY INTERESTS
OF CARL HASTINGS MILAM

Carl Milam's interest in the United Nations Library, of which he was director from 1948 to 1950, was a natural outgrowth of a life-long interest in libraries all over the world. During World War I and thereafter (from 1917 to 1920) he served as assistant director of the Library War Service, sponsored by the American Library Association. In 1920, he became the executive secretary of the Association. During his twenty-eight years and one month as executive secretary of the A. L. A., Milam frequently visited libraries in foreign countries and participated in many international library activities. Some of these activities were sponsored by A. L. A. or were programs of the International Relations Board and the International Relations Office of A. L. A. Other activities resulted from invitations by national and international agencies, such as the United States Department of State and UNESCO.

In 1920, the year Milam became executive secretary, the American Library in Paris was opened. This library grew out of the central headquarters library of A. L. A. 's Library War Service in Paris. Because of public interest in the library after the war, A. L. A. agreed to leave the collection of 25,000 volumes and the library equipment, and to donate an endowment of $25,000 to provide some funding. Local private financial support was obtained to provide additional funding in order to maintain the library on a continuing basis. The library is still in existence, and it is now governed by a Board of Trustees of twenty-four members, five of whom are nominated by A. L. A.

Carl Milam worked closely with Sarah Bogle, the director of the Paris Library School, which was also sponsored by A. L. A. and which lasted five years, from 1924 to 1929. The school was closed for lack of financial support.

Milam attended the organizational meetings of the In-

ternational Federation of Library Associations in Prague in
1926 and in Edinburgh in 1927. In 1929, 1931, 1933, and
1935 he was a delegate to the International Library Congresses
in Rome, Cheltenham (England), Chicago, and in Madrid and
Barcelona respectively. While in Europe in 1946 he attended
a meeting of the International Federation of Library Associations called for the purpose of reactivating the Federation
after the war.

Besides being active in this international library organization, he was an honorary member of the Asociación de
Bibliotecarios y Bibliógrafos de España, a corresponding member of the Academia Nacional de Ciencias Antonio Alzate of
Mexico, and a "locio honorario" of the Asociación de Bibliotecarios Ecuatorianos.

In 1938, Milam became a member of the advisory
committee of the Division of Cultural Relations of the Department of State. This division (since 1945 called the Bureau
of Educational and Cultural Affairs) was responsible for the
distribution to other countries of representative writings about
the United States. In 1939, Milam spoke before the Inter-
American Bibliographical and Library Association meeting in
Washington, D.C., about the possibility of cooperation among
the libraries of the United States and Latin America.

In August and September, 1941, he visited Mexico City
with Marion A. Milczewski, his assistant, for the purpose of
working out a plan of action for the establishment of the Benjamin Franklin Library in Mexico, the second American library
to be established in a foreign country. On April 13, 1942,
he returned to Mexico City for the dedication of the library.
The establishment of this library was made possible by a
grant from the Coordinator of Inter-American Affairs to the
American Library Association.

Milam visited Latin America again in June, July, and
August of 1944, this time with Harry M. Lydenberg, director
of the International Relations Office of the American Library
Association. They visited the American libraries in Mexico
City, Managua, and Montevideo, and evaluated the library
school programs in Bogotá, Quito, Lima, and São Paulo.

Milam served as one of three American Council on
Education consultants to the U.S. Department of State during
the United Nations Conference on International Organization
held in San Francisco in April and May, 1945. His name,

CARL HASTINGS MILAM

however, is not mentioned in connection with the fledgling
United Nations Library established in San Francisco to serve
the delegates to the conference.

On December 27, 1946, Milam reported to the Midwinter Meeting of A. L. A. on a six-week trip to Europe where
he served, at the invitation of the Department of State, as a
library consultant to the U. S. Delegation to UNESCO. As a
member of the Library and Museums Subcommittee, he worked
out a dozen brief proposals which were used as the basis of

a report submitted for action.   The main features of the library program proposed by the Subcommittee were: (1) promotion of public libraries throughout the world, (2) removal of barriers to the free flow of publications across national boundaries, (3) stimulation of the production of bibliographies, indexes, and union catalogs, and (4) development of a good library for the UNESCO Secretariat.

Milam attended a regional meeting of UNESCO in Philadelphia in April, 1947; and a meeting in September, 1947, in Chicago, of the U.S. National Commission for UNESCO.   This commission, composed of one hundred American citizens, was a link between UNESCO and organizations and individuals in the United States concerned with education, science, and culture.

It comes as no surprise then to discover that early in 1947, Carl Milam evinced an interest in the United Nations Library, which had opened in Hunter College in New York City when the United Nations first met there and which later was moved to Lake Success along with the United Nations Secretariat.   Milam was aware of the work of William Warner Bishop and the League of Nations Library Planning Committee, an advisory group of librarians from many countries. In the spring of 1947, he suggested that a similar group be formed to advise the United Nations Library.   He also offered his assistance to the United Nations Library in the capacity of a consultant.   He was asked instead to become a member of a committee which conducted the first of many surveys that were undertaken during the next decade of United Nations Library activities.   Besides Milam, the committee included Ralph A. Beals, Luther H. Evans, and Arthur C. Breycha-Vauthier.   These four men spent two days at the United Nations, April 22 and 23, 1947, and wrote a report recommending some guidelines that the Library should follow.   (See Appendix A.)

On January 22, 1948, Milam received a telegram from Benjamin Cohen, assistant secretary-general of the Department of Public Information, that was to change the course of his professional life.   A day or two later he received a letter asking him to serve as a full-time consultant to the United Nations Library.   Further negotiations were conducted and on May 1, 1948, Milam became an official of the United Nations Secretariat with the title of Director of the Division of Library Services and with a salary of $10,000.

Between January and May, Milam had undergone many days of soul-searching regarding his change of position, for it was difficult for him to leave a position after twenty-eight years. There were both advantages and disadvantages to consider. When he visited the library in 1947 and 1948 he had recognized its weaknesses in service and administration. He was aware, however, of the causes behind the unsatisfactory conditions and was optimistic that these conditions would respond to his direction.

Somehow sensing that the years of 1948 to 1950 would be momentous, he started a journal, published in this volume, which he labeled "CHM's Diary on U. N. " The first entry in the diary is dated February 7, 1948, some twenty days before he finally accepted the new position. Assured by Secretariat officials that they would support good library service, at the end of February, at the age of sixty-three, he plunged into planning for a new and challenging job--at an age at which most men are making plans for retirement.

His first step was to spend part of the week from March 9 to March 12, 1948, in New York, serving as a consultant to the library. He met with the library staff, and agreement was reached on the following: provision of an aggressive library service to the Secretariat, development of a legislative reference type of service for the Secretariat personnel and delegates, the offering of limited research service for outsiders, acquisition of a currently useful collection, and maximum utilization of the services of other New York libraries. (See Appendix C.)

Milam was on the United Nations payroll from May 1, 1948, but actually reported to work on May 4. His arrival marked the beginning of two of the most exciting years in the history of the United Nations Library. They were also very rewarding years for Carl Milam.

The diary consists of only sixty-six entries and covers a period from January, 1948, through June, 1950. Twenty-seven of the entries were written before Milam officially assumed his duties as director. They reflect his concern for salary, housing, and moving. Meetings with United Nations officials to determine general library policy were also recorded. The remainder of the entries include nine for 1948, fifteen for 1949, and fifteen for 1950. During Milam's two years as director, his chief concerns were budget and personnel. He frequently bemoaned the lack of time to write

and mentioned his "poor neglected diary." Finding solutions
to the many problems became more and more frustrating to
him, and he reported dreaming about his work.

The successes were also noted in the diary. These
included a reorganization of services, the drafting and acceptance of an official policy statement for the library, the
meeting of the International Advisory Committee of Library
Experts, the establishment of an internship program, the ini-
tiation of the United Nations Documents Index, the first annual
report of the library, the transfer of the library to the office
of the Secretary-General from the Department of Public Information, the receipt of the Woodrow Wilson Memorial Library, preparation for moving the library to the Manhattan
building next to the new United Nations buildings, and the reclassification and subsequent upgrading of professional positions. This last accomplishment was considered by Joseph
Groesbeck, deputy director of the United Nations Library from
1956 to 1970, as Milam's most important accomplishment.

On April 4, 1950, Milam wrote in his diary that he
would probably stay at the United Nations until November 1,
although his two-year contract was scheduled to expire on
May 1, 1950. However, on June 28, he penned the following
brief note: "Incidentally my last pay day." Although he gave
no reason in the diary for his sudden change of mind, his
wife's poor health was probably a deciding factor.

In addition to delineating the administrative details
and frustrations encountered in running a library, Milam
wrote in his diary of personal events. He wrote about the
opening of the trout season, the garden show in New York,
his thirty-eighth wedding anniversary, and the polo games on
Long Island. He spoke about the Secretary-General and other
United Nations officials as well as the clerks and secretaries.

After his retirement, Carl Milam and his wife, Nell,
returned to the farm near Barrington, Illinois, which they
had bought some years earlier. They grew irises and apples
and Christmas trees. He nursed his wife tenderly through
the slow encroachments of a progressively worsening disease
until she died in 1956.

Professional concerns occupied some of his time after
formally retiring. In 1953 he wrote a lengthy article on the
United Nations Library for Library Quarterly (see Appendix
F). In 1954 Milam was elected an honorary life member of

the American Library Association. The A. L. A. Executive
Board in its minutes of June 20-25, 1954, stated: "The development of American libraries abroad as instruments of
international information and good will was due primarily to
his continued interest and effective negotiation with philan-
thropic organizations and governmental agencies. "

After his wife's death, when the garden work became
too difficult, he began to work on a book with Helen Wessells.
The book was to be a compilation of articles on librarianship
which would show library work as the thrilling, challenging
adventure he had always found it to be. Although some chap-
ters were completed, the book was never finished.

In late 1961, just before his tragic death, the Secretary-General of the United Nations, Dag Hammarskjöld, invited Carl Hastings Milam and other dignitaries to attend the
dedication of the new library building of the United Nations.
Milam attended the dedication on November 16, 1961, along
with three other former U. N. librarians. A two-day sym-
posium held following the dedication was concluded by a tribute from Verner Clapp to Andrew Cordier. In this tribute
Clapp spoke of the contribution Carl Milam had made to the
organization, functioning and continuing direction of the library, which would henceforth be called the Dag Hammarskjöld Library.

Within two years after his return to Illinois, Milam
sold his farm and made plans to move to Jamaica, Iowa, to
be near his daughter. The move was never completed. He
died at home in Barrington, Illinois, on August 26, 1963, at
the age of 78.

In 1971 the Carl H. Milam Memorial Lecture was established by the American Library Association. The first
lecture was given on May 18, 1971, by Herman Liebaers,
director of the Royal Library in Brussels and president of the
International Federation of Library Associations. The topic
of Liebaers' lecture was "Librarianship and International Relations, " a fitting tribute to Carl Hastings Milam.

Doris Cruger Dale
Southern Illinois University at
Carbondale, Illinois

October, 1975

INTERNATIONAL LIBRARIANSHIP:

A BIBLIOGRAPHY OF
PUBLISHED WRITINGS BY MILAM

"The Benjamin Franklin Library Dedication. " A. L. A. Bulletin, vol. 36, no. 5 (May, 1942), pp. 312-314.

"The Depository Library System. " United Nations Bulletin, vol. 6, no. 6 (March 15, 1949), pp. 273-275.

"Libraries of the United States and Canada, 1931-32. " International Federation of Library Associations. Publications, vol. 4 (1932), pp. 114-121.

"Libraries of the United States and Canada, 1933-35. " International Federation of Library Associations. Publications, vol. 7 (1935), pp. 72-80.

"Libraries, Scholars, and the War. " The Annals of the American Academy of Political and Social Science, vol. 235 (September, 1944), pp. 100-106.

"Library Participation in International Cultural Relations. " A. L. A. Bulletin, vol. 36, no. 2 (February, 1942), pp. 76-77.

"Notes on the Visit to Latin America. " A. L. A. Bulletin, vol. 38, no. 8 (September, 1944), pp. 299-300.

"Some Possibilities of Library Cooperation with Latin America. " A. L. A. Bulletin, vol. 33, no. 4 (April, 1939), pp. 227-231.

"UNESCO: Its Program as a Whole. " Canadian Library Association Bulletin, vol. 3, no. 6 (June 1947), p. 141.

"UNESCO's Library Program. " A. L. A. Bulletin, vol. 41, no. 2 (February, 1947), pp. 35-38.

"The United Nations Library." The Library Quarterly, vol. 23, no. 4 (October, 1953), pp. 267-280.

"Visit to Latin America." A. L. A. Bulletin, vol. 38, no. 6 (June, 1944), pp. 229-230.

"Work of the Library Committee." United Nations Bulletin, vol. 5, no. 5 (September 1, 1948), pp. 681-682.

"CHM'S DIARY ON U. N. "

New York, February 7, 1948[1]*

Wonder if I'll ever write in it again after today! I attended the San Francisco Conference for about 2 weeks in 1945, as an educational consultant. I went as consultant on libraries to the Unesco conference in Paris, November, 1946. Regional U. S. meeting on Unesco, April, 1947, Philadelphia. National Commission for Unesco, Chicago, September, 1947.

ADVISORY COMMITTEE

In the spring of 1947, following letters from me to [Arthur] Sweetser [director, United Nations Information Center in Washington] and from Luther Evans [Librarian of Congress] to Byron Price [assistant secretary-general for Administrative and Financial Services] (at my suggestion) proposing an international library advisory committee, Evans, [Ralph] Beals [director, New York Public Library], and I were invited to spend 2 days at Lake Success and New York City. [Arthur C.] Breycha-Vauthier [librarian, United Nations Library, Geneva] was brought over for the discussions. Mr. Pelt of Holland, Adrian Pelt, Assistant Secretary-General for Conference and General Services, in whose department the library was then operated, was our principal host. Mr. [François] Stefanini [director, Bureau of Technical Services] was with

*See Notes, beginning on page 71.

1

us most of the time. [2]

We conferred with many people, including the architects, and made the recommendations which follow[3] [see Appendix A].

[Verner W.] Clapp [director of Acquisitions Department, Library of Congress] and [John E.] Burchard [director of libraries, Massachusetts Institute of Technology] were engaged as we proposed, and later made valuable reports. [4]

Later, in the summer or autumn, [Ralph] Shaw [librarian, U.S. Department of Agriculture] was engaged to do the library part of a management study and produced a report of more than 100 pages [see Appendix B], which has been severely criticized but which appears to contain more useful as well as some--very likely--unreliable information. [5] His employment had no connection with the advisory committee.

January 22, 1948

Received telegram from Ben Cohen [assistant secretary-general, Department of Public Information] asking me [to] give favorable consideration to letter which would follow.

January 23 or 24, 1948

Received letter. [6]

January 24, 1948

Replied.

January 29 or 30, 1948

Received his [Cohen's reponse] letter of January 28 at Edgewater Beach Hotel during Midwinter Conference. Arranged to be in New York February 5. Letters and telegrams follow.

February 5, 1948

Cohen and V. Stavridi (V. J. G. Stavridi, director of division in "Reference & Publication"--U. K.) picked me up in a U. N. car and we drove to Lake Success.

He (Cohen) was very cordial, hoped I would decide to help them out. I recall conversation about the great library resources of New York City, the meeting he had recently attended (called by [Raymond] Fosdick [president and trustee of the Rockefeller Foundation] and [Devereaux C.] Josephs [president and trustee, Carnegie Corporation], and attended by university presidents and Hadley [Morris, president, Board of Trustees, New York Public Library] and Beals) for beginning discussions of library coordination.

He and Stavridi and I spent an hour in his office in two sessions. They explained the present set-up for library service and what I could do for it.

My first major jobs would be to establish a library policy, and to complete the integration of the several units which have now been united (on paper) in the Department of Information.

I was assured that I would have a free hand within the budget and of course the general regulations.

The staff is now 54 or 56 and must be reduced to 51. Most are on temporary appointment and can be discharged on 30-day notice. Some are "permanent" but they too can be discharged. Personnel Department is cooperative.

Whether the Geneva Library would come under my supervision appears not to have been determined.

Stavridi gave me the approximate budget figures as follows:

```
For salaries--51 or 54 ?                $206,607
   Acquisitions, N.Y.                     96,600
   Geneva                                 22,000  Acqui-
                                                  sitions
Information Centers (6 or 7)              10,400
International Committee of
   Library Experts                        11,000
For contracts                             20,000
                                        $366,607
```

High salaries are:
```
   [Sigurd Hartz] Rasmussen [librarian]      7850
   [Edouard] Reitman [chief, Reference
      Center, Department of Public
      Information]                            6700
   [John] Perry [assistant librarian]        6700
Next level is                                4900
```

Most of the "allowances" come from other funds.

In discussing the International Committee of Library Experts we had in mind 5 persons:

U.S.S.R. --1 if possible

Western Europe--[Julien] Cain [director, National Library of France], or [Pierre] Bourgeois [director, Swiss National Library], or [Lionel R.] McColvin [city librarian, Westminster, England], or [Frank] Francis [keeper of the Department of Printed Books, the British Museum]

Latin America--[Ernesto G.] Gietz [Institute of Library Science, University of Buenos Aires] or [Carlos V.] Penna [University of Buenos Aires] or [Jorge] Basadre [director, Department of Cultural Affairs, Pan American Union]

U.S. --Evans

China or India--one

Cohen spoke of a possible meeting 3 or 4 months after I begin, possibly a 15-day meeting. He hopes committee will discuss, among other things, how U.N. library can help other libraries; and I added, and how other libraries can help U.N. to be known and understood.

I mentioned Rubens Borba de Moraes [director, National Library of Brazil] as a possible permanent librarian. Much interest. Brazil would be a good country for such person to come from. Stavridi brought this up later. He or John McDiarmid [chief, Staff Regulations Division, Department of Administrative and Financial Services] asked if he and I would work well together if he were brought in fairly soon as my deputy and I said yes.

There is a Library Committee composed of 1 person from each department. It is presumably advisory.

I was told that I could have a professional assistant and a secretary. They may have to come from present library staff. Perry, who is now Rasmussen's assistant, was mentioned as a possibility with some reservations....

I took particular pains to say 2 or 3 times that I would need the advice of experts on many technical matters, such as building planning, indexing, microfilms, etc., and was told that could be arranged.

Before I left with Stavridi and his secretary, Miss [Dorothy] Compton [later to become Milam's secretary], in a U.N. car, I told Cohen I wanted to be assured that [Secretary-General Trygvie] Lie, as the big boss, and Byron Price, as the budget boss, wanted good library service. I did not ask for specific commitments, but only for general assurances.

Cohen answered me, in effect, that he would back me up, and I could leave everything to him. (See notes on McDiarmid and conferences, February 6).[7]

Rasmussen and Reitman were called to Stavridi's office and we went to the lounge for conversation and much of the talk was about the Shaw report which they (especially Rasmussen) don't like, about the requests for books outside the library's scope, about the difficulty of depending on short-time loans from other libraries, etc. --Rasmussen doing most of the talking.

. . .

Stavridi joined us for lunch.

Then we visited the unimpressive looking library in 2 or 3 different places.

For some reason which I could not take in, the library in using 2 classification systems. [8]

I met Perry but was not introduced to any other staff members.

Rasmussen came to the Algonquin and talked for 3 hours more. Much the same. But I still think he may be usable somehow.

John McDiarmid came along late afternoon at my request and was very helpful.

Cohen had suggested 2 alternatives.
Consultant basis, $50 per day for days worked, no vacation, no tax exemption;
or
Salary of $10,000, in effect, tax free.

I preferred the latter and any discussion with John was on that basis.

It appears to come out like this: See also February 9.

Salary 1st year	10,000
Salary 2d year	10,500
Allowances:	
Moving (man and wife and goods)	500
Rental, 600 + 600?	? 1,200*--?
60 day living allowance	
420 for me, 210 for wife	630
Installation	200
Two years - - - - - - - - - - - - - -	23,030

*Rental allowance is 25% of rent but not over 6% of base salary.

U.N. will pay income tax this year (1948); may or

may not next year. But any change will probably mean an increase in salary.

U.N. has a pension scheme, 14% by employee, 7% by employer. Would probably be willing to take over A.L.A.'s part in Metropolitan A.L.A. plan.

This is to be compared with:

A.L.A. salary, 2 years	$24,000
Less Income tax, say	4,500
	19,500

23,030 - 19,500 = 3,530 for 2 years
1,765 for each year

Thus there would apparently be $1,765 per year to pay increased costs in New York.

Note. Some of the U.N. figures are still uncertain.

If 2-year contract runs from May 1, I would work 1 month longer than if I remained in Chicago, and then would collect 1 extra salary check of about $875.

For security, A.L.A. is a slightly better bet. As preparation for possible jobs after retirement, take U.N. See February 9.

In answer to my question McDiarmid said I could trust Cohen to back up my proposals, but he would probably be backing several other proposals at the same time.

Walter Kotschnig [U.S. alternate representative, U.N. General Assembly, Seventh Session] came over to where we were sitting in the lounge. When I told him my story, he advised definite commitments as to space and funds--which I rejected. As I did his offer of a "quick one"--because I didn't have time and had already had a scotch on John McDiarmid.

Living Arrangements. All agree it is difficult to find house or apartment in New York or Long Island.

U.N. has a housing bureau and controls some apartments.

February 6, 1948

Beals. Talked with him in his office for about an hour. He wants me to take the job. Assures me full cooperation New York Public Library within the limitations of the charter, which are considerable. He spoke briefly of the interlibrary lending problems; of the proposal to establish an international center and branch (NYPL) library adjacent to the U.N. site; of the recent meeting on coordination of resources and another one coming next week.

From his office I telephoned for Fosdick, who was out of city; talked with [John] Marshall [Rockefeller Foundation], and saw him at 10:45.

Telephoned Alger Hiss [president, Carnegie Endowment for International Peace], made date for 2:10. Telephoned Carl White [director of libraries, Columbia University, and dean, Columbia University School of Library Service]. Out.

John Marshall, Rockefeller Foundation. Reported briefly, stated problem. Fosdick might be able to help. Marshall will explain and I can call him next Wednesday at 2 p.m. Chicago time. He thought Fosdick wouldn't have much information about attitude of Lie and Price, but might have ways of finding out, possibly through Sweetser.

Asked about [T. P.] Sevensma [permanent secretary, International Federation of Library Associations] and I told all I knew. [9]

Robert M. Lester, C.C. [secretary, Carnegie Corporation]. Saw him at 12 and he and Memory [Lester's wife] took me to dinner. He thinks it is a great thing for me to get out of A.L.A. before my time is up; that I can do a good job for U.N.

Best remark of the week: "What a backfield! We could lick the Wolverines."

Alger Hiss, Carnegie Endowment. It was my first meeting with him. He is constantly in close touch with U.N. officials. He has discussed library with Price, and could assure me that Price is opposed to building up a great collection. Hiss would guess that he favors good library service. At my request agreed to call Andrew W. Cordier (U.S.A.), executive assistant to the Secretary-General.

Later Hiss telephoned that Cordier says Lie is thoroughly convinced of need for good library service and of making full use of other library resources.

Hiss suggested I ask Cohen to go with me to see Price about the attitude of Committee 5, which is the budget committee. I did not act on this suggestion, but found a better way, as explained next page.

Hiss asked me whether I thought U.N. library could be housed across the street in proposed combined international center and New York Public Library branch library. I was doubtful. He asked me to speak with Beals about it.

He seemed to think that decision had been made to use the Manhattan Building for a library. It is a small 7-story office building on the U.N. site. Intimated Wally Harrison [director of planning, Headquarters Planning Office] had suggested its use to avoid necessity of providing library quarters in U.N. office building.

Mentioned appointment of a Mr. [R.G.A.] Jackson [senior deputy director-general] of UNRRA [United Nations Relief and Rehabilitation Administration] as a new deputy secretary-general at large under Lie, and didn't know whether that would change Price's position as boss of the budget--my words.

Carl White. Brief conversation on telephone in which he assured me again how eager he is to have me take over at U.N.

Luther Evans, long distance. I explained briefly. He volunteered to call Price. Later he called back to be sure Price had called me, said he was "awfully happy" at the way things were going. Library of Congress will give me maximum support.

Byron Price. Telephoned saying Luther had called explaining I wanted some assurances. He had talked with Cohen. They were agreed "we want a reference and research service which is the best in the world and that we don't want to duplicate the New York Public Library." The secretariat will sympathetically support good library service. Of course U.N. must operate within budgets set by the delegates but he finds them--the Committee of 5--normally interested and sympathetic.

Bob Lester was in the room when this very important word came. So we had a drink on it.

February 7, 1948[10]

Paul North Rice [chief, Reference Department, New York Public Library, and president, A. L. A.]. Came over for lunch. I explained the situation to him. He wishes it weren't happening while he is president. I suggested he write [E. W.] McDiarmid [librarian, University of Minnesota, and president-elect, A. L. A.] how things are going so that he can begin to think hard about my successor. I agreed to keep him posted.

I explained that one thing might prevent my acceptance, namely financial terms; and that one might prevent an offer, namely my nationality.

Summary, February 9, 1948

    The Library, as of now, is a poor thing. The many pieces have not been put together, the physical arrangements leave much to be desired, the staff is said to be divided, and I'm sure the service to readers isn't good.

    These unsatisfactory conditions are probably due to many causes, including:

        Lack of library policy.

        Divided resources, personnel, authority.

        General confusion resulting from building a big outfit quickly.

        Necessity to employ many nationalities.

        Relatively weak direction. . . .

        Pessimism, resistance to change, stubborn enforcement of rules, poor public relations.

        Shaw's report was upsetting.

    These conditions will not be easily corrected, but I think they will respond to such devices as:

        Staff meetings for the discussion of policies and improvements, possibly followed by working committees, on general library policy, integration of the several units into a system, space arrangements, the Shaw report.

        Meetings of the Library Committee.

        Meetings with New York librarians.

        Advice of specialists.

        Adequate justification of the budget requests.

        Good relations with key people in Secretariat.

Reasons for accepting	Reasons against
1. There's an important job to be done.	1. It is easier just to stay put.

2. My friends think I
   should do it.
3. Good way to top off career.
4. It will increase prospects
   for future part-time jobs of
   interest to me.
5. I may be able to do a little
   to increase usefulness of
   U.N.
6. I know of no one who would
   be in a better position to do
   the job that needs to be
   done.
7. Assurances from Cohen,
   Price and Cordier (for Lie)
   that they want good library
   service.
8. The good "backfield."

2. Many uncertainties as to
   achieving a satisfactory
   degree of success.
3. Upsetting Margery [a
   daughter].
4. Distance from Jamaica
   [Iowa, home of another
   daughter, Mary, Mrs.
   William A. Seidler, Jr.]
   and Oklahoma [reared
   and educated there].
5. Distance from farm [his
   21 acres near Barring-
   ton, Ill.].
6. Expense of trips to farm
   for vacation or what have
   you.
7. May be able to save
   less in New York.
8. It requires Executive
   Board to make quick
   decision about my suc-
   cessor.
9. If I were to become ill,
   A.L.A. would be more
   likely to care for me.

INCOME

Salary U.N. 2 years		$20,500
Salary A.L.A.	24,000	
Less income tax	4,500	
		19,500

Excess U.N. over A.L.A.	1,000
Excess U.N. over A.L.A. 1 year	500

Assuming the allowances other than rent ($1330) pay the
costs they are supposed to cover.

Assuming that rent would cost $1800.
That rental allowance is $450.
Our excess of New York rent over Evanston rent would
be $810.
    1800 - 450 = 1350
    1350 - 540 = $810
This is $310 more than the excess of U.N. over A.L.A.
income*

If other living costs are up $50 a month the loss is increased to $910 per year. †
    *But if rental is $2400 and rental allowance is $600 our excess cost for rent would be $760.
†and possible total loss, $1360.

All this assumes U. N. would take over A. L. A.'s share of my annuity payments.

These losses would be offset in part by one more month's salary of $875 for April, 1950. But this would probably no more than cover expense of moving back to Barrington.

If income tax is reduced, I would stand to lose the benefit of that reduction.

February 10, 1948

    I reported the essential facts to the Heads of Departments at A. L. A.

February 11, 1948

    Raymond Fosdick, Rockefeller Foundation. As agreed last week I called him long distance at 2 p. m. Chicago time. John Marshall had reported to him and he had seen my letter of February 9 to John.

    "Great opportunity. Hope you can do it. Some personnel difficulties. Cohen is a facile kind of person. Speaks well. Not too experienced as an administrator. Intentions are good. Sincere. Deeply in earnest. "

    Fosdick then spoke of the meeting to discuss library coordination which Cohen had attended.

    "Sincerely hope you will take it. It would mean a great deal to the coordination of libraries in the New York area. "

    He advised me to talk with Sweetser.

Arthur Sweetser, U.N. Information Office, Washington.
He says I would have complete support of Secretariat.
Question is about the delegates--how generous they are. That,
in turn, will depend on economic conditions and the attitude
of governments.

He agrees the library is a mess. Everything thrown
together. No organization, policy or method. People want
something good.

Cohen was librarian at National Library in Chile for
5 years and fancies himself in that role. He has wanted the
library in his department and has worked to that end, because of his library experience and because he thinks library
should be an agency to serve the general public (or perhaps
a special public--CHM) as well as the Secretariat. Sweetser
disagrees somewhat on that latter, thinking library must put
needs of Secretariat first (and so do I). Not too serious.
Because of this conception the Library may have a larger
role than otherwise.

Bureaucracy is worse than Geneva. I must expect
difficulties in getting decisions.

He then spoke of the discussions about an independent
research center and 16 big universities getting together trying
to build a center, based on the Geneva Research Center, for
scholars and students. (This may be the same thing Beals
and Alger Hiss talked about.)

This is all a part of the show, of the intellectual life
and organization growing up around the United Nations.

There is also the League Library at Geneva.

"Cohen will be your best support. Imagination. Great
stimulator, not much on details. Will probably expect you to
run your own show."

"Price will be next best."

"Lie, away up there, is not an intellectual in any
sense. He is a political fellow. Is likely to judge by what
people--especially delegates--say about the library. Quick
and temperamental."

It would be a big job. Evans suggested my name to
Sweetser and he passed it on to Cohen. The suggestion was
immediately accepted. His reasons for endorsing me were
three: 1. Neutrality--not connected with New York Public
Library or Library of Congress or Harvard, etc. 2. International interests over a long period. 3. The right age to
tackle one more good job. He thinks I could do the job and
hopes I will.

I said it now depends on terms and he was most encouraging about finding not too expensive housing. Said there
were all sorts of places--even chauffeurs could afford to live
out there!

February 12, 1948

I have finished reading Shaw's management study of
U.N. Library services. It is full of useful information and
suggestions. But I must and will be on my guard, knowing
how unreliable Shaw's statements are.

February 25, 1948

12 noon. I am sitting here in the Hotel Washington
waiting for the letter which was to come "concurrently."

Mildred Batchelder [school and children's libraries
specialist, A.L.A.] telephoned [Edna V.] Vanek [assistant
editor, A.L.A. Booklist] in Chicago at my request, Monday
about 11 [?]. Was informed that a letter from U.N. [11] was
at hand and would be air mailed to me in Washington. It
has not arrived. But a letter from Nell [Milam's wife],

mailed about the same time reached me at 9, February 24, Tuesday.

I decided at 4:45 to wait for it. Having just telephoned Mrs. [Gwendolen B.] White [Milam's secretary at A. L. A. headquarters in Chicago] who said the letter had been sent, that she would telephone me if she discovered anything screwy.

And here I sit.

Shall I ask Lake Success to send a copy?

2 p. m. The letter arrived, and I was not called! Found it in my box about 1:20. It reached the hotel at 12:57. Delay was apparently due to failure to attach new stamps.

> Salary $10,000.
> Income tax for 1948 reimbursed or paid by U. N.
> Personal transportation and moving expenses.
> U. N. will take over A. L. A. annuity payment.
> $250 for hospitality in 1948.
> 2 Bedroom U. N. apartments, unfurnished, $117.
> 25% of rent up to $50.00.
> No mention of 60 day living allowance, 630
>   Installation   200

Shall I ask about these items? $830 is a lot of money. Also about 2d year salary?

Sunday, February 29, 1948

I am a little limp after the great decision. Maybe Nell is too but she doesn't show it. We are both overwhelmed at the thought of getting a place to live, packing, storing, moving, deciding what to do with the farm, helping Margery decide whether to go or stay.

On Friday (27th) I telephoned Rice and McDiarmid, wrote Executive Board, Beals and Rice about need for living quarters. Also a separate letter to U.N. on this subject.

On Saturday I wrote to Dick [Luther L. Dickerson, formerly librarian, Indianapolis Public Library, and a close

friend] and C. E. R. [Charles E. Rush, director, University
of North Carolina Library], and I told Charlie Brown [li-
brarian emeritus, Iowa State College]. He was surprised,
glad for my own sake, but feared Ralph Shaw might cause
more trouble in my absence.

McDiarmid, [Amy] Winslow [assistant director, Enoch
Pratt Free Library, Baltimore] and [Elizabeth D.] Briggs
[director of work with children, Cleveland Public Library]
are the Executive Board Committee to find my successor.
McDiarmid suggests asking Divisions and staff to assist,
which I think is a good idea. [Everett O.] Fontaine [chief,
Publishing Department, A. L. A.] has been alerted. [Paul]
Howard [Washington Office, A. L. A.] and [Helen E.] Wessells
[acting director, A. L. A. International Relations Office,
Washington] informed.

March 1, 1948

Letter from Rice. He had been in touch with Cohen,
implied public announcement will be made soon.

I told [Sydney H.] Kasper [account executive] of Mit-
chell McKeown who said he would telephone or telegraph
Cohen asking for copy of release to be used by Kasper in
Chicago.

I told Mrs. [Margaret Ritchie] Post [editor, A. L. A.
Bulletin] and prepared a brief signed "Bulletin from the corner office" to be used with March Bulletin if U. N. makes
announcement soon.

Arthur Sweetser. Came in for a visit, no special
business. Was pleased I'd accepted.

He had been talking with Rotary International about
some scholarships they had provided. $7500, I think it was.
Which, with $3000 from Carnegie Endowment and $3000 from

Carnegie Corporation through Carnegie Endowment, will make it possible for 40 people to spend a month at U.N. this summer. National governments are expected to provide transportation.

He said very little effort had been made to interest foundations. (Maybe this is where I come in.)

He spoke at some length of the proposed university center and international organizations center. Indicated, I think, that they might be combined. Seemed not to have heard of New York Public Library branch in this connection. Agreed with me the building, off U.N. property, could not properly be used for U.N. library. Spoke of his proposal to Woodrow Wilson Foundation that it dispose of its library, preferably not to U.N. but to the center outside. This would greatly reduce the foundation's annual expense. Might (not quite sure about this) enable foundation to use its assets for or toward the erection of building for this center as a monument to Wilson. Said Wally Harrison is very much interested in the architectural development of the area adjacent to U.N. property.

He had learned that U.N. library does not have reports of the League Library Planning Committee, and he has arranged to have photostat copies sent to Lake Success.

Thought we ought to assume U.S.S.R. would be represented on Library Advisory Committee.

. . .

I asked Sweetser about relations with Unesco. He implied they were slightly strained--because in certain fields U.N. and Unesco are both attempting to operate. He thought Unesco's program amorphous, too all-embracing.

Stavridi is a good guy, Greek extraction, British. Had been director of London office. Uncertain of his future.

Trained as a lawyer.   May be sent to some outpost.   Pulled off now for work with children's fund.

March 2, 1948

Rice reports by telephone that Cohen has not yet received my acceptance.   Rice agreed to call [Mary G.] Smieton [director of Personnel] and to let me know if my letter failed to reach her.   Cohen hopes Rice won't spread the news yet.   Kasper was going to call Cohen from here today sometime.   No report from him.

I told Angus Macdonald [president, Snead and Co., Orange, Va.] the news.   He thought it was swell.

March 9, 1948

Arrived Algonquin about 8:45 a.m.   See Cohen telegram March 3.[12]   Found note saying car would arrive for me at 9:30.   It did.   Also found letter of March 8 from Clapp and Evans.[13]   See preceding pages.

Transportation.   Driver of car says Directors and Assistant Secretaries-General may have a car any time they want it, day or night; that I can be driven to and from Lake Success every day if I wish!   I wonder?

Cohen.   Called to Washington.   Back tomorrow.

Janecek, George, Executive Officer [Department of Public Information].   I was taken to him.   He welcomed me and we had a long talk, part of it with his assistant whose name I didn't get.[14]

. . .

In addition to personnel there are problems of space, reorganization.

We agreed that service should be first to the Secretariat and that Cohen should be protected or prevented from talking too much about service to public.

I looked over the manning table and discovered 4, instead of 2, top people: [H.J.] Timperley [acting director of library services] (Australia), Research; [Karel] Naprstek [chief] (Opinion survey); Rasmussen; Reitman.

Shaw report has not been seen by staff. Distribution would infer approval, and it hasn't been approved as a whole.

[Tor] Gjesdal [principal director, Department of Public Information]. Not sure of full name or title, but he appears to be the no. 2 man in Cohen's department. Norwegian of course and knows [Wilhelm] Munthe [librarian, University of Oslo] and [Arne] Kildal [library adviser, Office of Adult Education, Ministry of Church and Education, Norway].

Seemed to agree with all that was said in the above conversation.

Also that it would be wise to talk about what we must do in the immediate future rather than to lay down long time policies, especially insofar as they are negative.

. . .

Timperley. Acting director.

. . .

Was inclined to agree that all questions of permanent appointment should be delayed for 3 months. Reitman's case is most pressing. His appointment still temporary but he doesn't much care. (Stavridi says he is under graded.)

He got a copy of Shaw report for Rasmussen.

Stavridi. I lunched with him and took care of the check. His status is uncertain. Says I may inherit Miss Compton temporarily. She is hoping for a higher grading (which she later confirmed).

We went over the attached list of questions which Timperley had prepared. [15]

Staff Meeting. I had requested and Timperley had

arranged a meeting in my temporary office at 4.

Present. Timperley, Naprstek, Rasmussen, Reitman.

First and mainly we discussed Library policy. It was more or less agreed that we should emphasize: Aggressive library service to secretariat, which will involve notices to secretariat of new items in their fields.

Development, as staff permits, of legislative reference type of service for secretariat and delegates.

But that the very useful Research service for outsiders should be continued and expanded, and

That the Opinion Surveys for staff and others is of great importance.

Every acquisition by gift should be challenged as to its probable value before processing.

Unused material should be discarded.

Develop best possible service from other New York libraries.

Items mentioned were: Complete bibliographic controls, Basic reference collection, Standard books on main subjects, Ask Departments to make recommendations, Receive documents from member countries, Bibliographies, Library catalogs, Reference material on current questions, Periodicals, Pamphlets, Processed publications.

I asked each of the 4 to come back at 11, March 10, with brief statement of policy for use as preamble to budget request.

Timperley explained his budget request very convincingly. More of that later.

I said--mostly to Rasmussen--from now on this group is going to proceed on the assumption that what we agree should be done will be done. I'm an incorrigible optimist.

Cohen back with Timperley and Miss Compton.

The former will go out with me at 9, Wednesday.

March 10, 1948

Cohen not yet in.   At 11 a.m. staff group again.

Documents.   The Documents Index group in my show was having a conference with Jerome Wilcox [librarian, City College, New York] Chairman, A.L.A. Documents Committee. I declined to participate but said Wilcox would speak my mind as well as his own.   That probably means an increase in staff and costs.   Question is: Is the unit efficient?

1:00 Lunch with Miss [Naomi] Osborne [personnel officer, Administrative Placement Section], Personnel.   Flexibility in budget.   Best chance is to ask for personnel wanted, in particular spots, as easiest to justify.   Then shift if you need to.   Employees can be engaged at other than minimum.

She asked for--and I have--references for Borba de Moraes.   Send other nominations.

Recommend, with restraint, what we need.

Contracts with persons--delay for a few months.   Review when I arrive.   No decisions until about August 1.

Personal (executive) assistant about Grade 8.

She's a swell gal and friend.

2 or 3-5:30.   Meeting with library group.   I met several members of the staff.   Good bunch.

6:00 Cocktail party for the Department of Public Information.   Met several new and old friends.

8:00 To Hotel with Stavridi (in his car), Compton, Timperley.

March 11, 1948

Worked in Hotel Room until about 1:00--on memorandum, mostly on policy, partly on budget.

Don't remember what I did 2-3.

3:00 Cohen   There wasn't much chance to present my observations; he had his own agenda.

Manhattan Building.   I must see it.   (I did not).   Temporary office - Manhattan office - 2nd floor available.   Use also as New York Information center.   See Glenn Bennett [executive officer, Headquarters Planning Office] and Wally Harrison.

Can we allow Military Committee to occupy top 2 floors for 10 years!   He thinks not.   I'm inclined to say yes.

At Lake Success we are using 12,600 square feet. Manhattan Building has (Eriksen) 10,000 feet per floor, 7 floors.   Four times present Lake Success Library space ought to be enough.   That means 5 floors and basement storage (CHM).

Can basement be used for storage needed now?   He understands moisture will prevent.

He hopes top floors will be available for director's office, research staff, cubicles for study, bibliography section.

Personnel.   Cohen intends I should have my own way.

. . .

Cohen returns May 20.

International Library Committee.   Have recommendations ready by May 20.   He does not object to meeting June 20 or early July.   Meeting could be June 20, or early July, and indicated need also for meeting of librarians of specialized agencies.

He would like to get Borba soon.   Gjesdal thinks maybe before January 1!

Director's Meeting, i.e., meeting of Directors of Department of Public Information.   Several things under consideration--not too important for me.

[Jan] Van Wijk [Bureau of Administrative Management and Budget][16] and [Spencer] Thompson [Department of Administrative and Financial Services]. I had appointment with former who took me in to Thompson's office for an hour's talk.

General impression: We are sitting pretty.

They didn't drop dead when I said we needed 50% increase in money for staff. Seemed to like my statement that book acquisitions be kept at around $100,000. They suspected some newspapers were being taken (at request of Secretariat) without cause.

. . .

They have not swallowed whole the management study.

"Don't think of us as enemies, but friends."

They aren't too worried about cuts made this year. They can be restored. Implication was I should ask for what I need, realizing increases won't be easy to get by the Advisory Committee and the 5th Committee.

They were very friendly and encouraging.

March 12, 1948

Byron Price. Arrived 10 minutes late because of ice on pavements.

Fine talk. Very understanding and sympathetic.

Called in [Rolv G.] Moltu [chief, Administrative Inspection Group, Department of Administrative and Financial Services], management expert.

Price said I should get acquainted with: Dr. (Mrs.) [Maria Z. N.] Witteveen [delegate] of Holland, Mr. [Roland] Lebeau [delegate] of Belgium, both of whom took particular interest in library budget for 1948.

I should see the minutes of the 5th Committee. Delegates fear Americanization. We must try to fill positions with other nationalities. Library staff not badly distributed but strong on those countries which are strong throughout the Secretariat: U.S., U.K., Scandinavia, Czechoslovakia. Weak on Brazil, Argentina.

. . .

Assistant Director from Brazil would be wonderful. No objection to my request for executive assistant.

Budget Policy 1948: 1st 4 grades--New York area; Grades 5-7, 75% New York area; Grades 8 up--Fair distribution.

As we left Moltu said "We'll get you your executive assistant."

I felt very encouraged as result of interview.

Library Committee. Cohen had said yes we should have a meeting. Gjesdal had called, and presided.

I reported on policy. No objection but considerable discussion.

I asked (twice) for criticisms and constructive suggestions about library service.

Friendly attitude. Can be useful. Should give them copies of my first memo.

Gjesdal. He wanted, and I gave, report on talks with Price and Thompson, as above.

Eriksen. Timperley and I reported talks with Price, Moltu, Thompson and Van Wijk, asking him not to kill our budget, if it requested increase, before it had gone to Budget authorities.

Timperley lunched with me. We went over budget and other library matters.

. . .

Photograph. I had my picture taken twice in the Reference room. Once with Reitman. For A.L.A. Bulletin.

Library Staff. Met with Timperley, Rasmussen, Reitman, and Naprstek to consider revision of memo. We were unable to conclude and I asked for written statements.

. . .

March 23, 1948

I'm already slipping. Much has happened since March 12, but I have not kept this diary. I can recall the following:

. . .

Manhattan Building. Gjesdal telephoned and we agreed that we probably could not justify library's immediate need for all 7 floors, that we should yield 2 top floors to the military committee for 5 years--not 10. I had previously written on this subject. Had said yes to the question about information space and a desk for me in that building.

. . .

New York Libraries. Wrote to several asking for description of services they had been called upon to render to U.N.

Shaw. Asked him for evaluation of people.

. . .

Staff Letter.[17] Next page [see Appendix C] sent through Timperley.

Return visit. Making plans for visit with Nell early April, 2 or 3 days for house hunting, one for business.

To March 31, 1948

Farewell reception by Library of International Relations, Chicago. Nice party. I made a brief speech which Nell said was O. K. It was a birthday party for her. Some of those present: Paul [U. S. senator from Illinois] and Emily Douglas, Mel [professor of anthropology, Northwestern University] and Frances Herskovits, George and Marian [former director, Evanston (Ill.) Public Library] Tomlinson, Herb [director, Public Administration Clearing House] and Mrs. Emmerich, Dr. [Winfred E.] Garrison [professor emeritus], University of Chicago and Cliff Dwellers [a Club], Ruth Savord [chief librarian, Council on Foreign Relations], Forrest Spaulding [librarian, Des Moines (Iowa) Public Library], Louis Nourse [assistant librarian, St. Louis Public Library], many local librarians, Herold Hunt [general superintendent of schools, Chicago], Miss Hall, teacher, Fred and Lucile Keck [she of Joint Reference Library, Public Administration Clearing House], Frank D. Loomis [secretary and executive director, Chicago Community Trust, and director, Community Fund of Chicago], Henry Moffat Yard, Judith Waller [director, Public Service and Education, Central Division, National Broadcasting Company].

I've conferred recently with Lucile Keck, Ruth Savord, and made some notes.

April 1, 1948

Conferred with [David R.] Kessler [librarian], Railroad Retirement Board Library.

. . .

April 8-10, 1948

Nell and I drove to New York.

April 10, 1948

Arrived Great Neck around 1 p. m. Mileage nearly

1000. Room ready soon at Colony House Hotel. Spent p. m.
looking around Long Island. [18]

. . .

April 11, 1948[19]

. . .

April 12, 1948

Now down to business. Called Mrs. [Mary] Hartigan
[administrative officer, Housing Section], United Nations,
Public Library, Timperley and Compton, and following real
estate agents: Murdoch, Allen and Stone; Edgar Storms;
Gray Sosa of Farmingdale.

Looked at apartments.

1 Maple Drive. 3 1/2 rooms, 1 bedroom. 3 years
5 months lease $135. No.

Academy Gardens. 5 rooms. 3 bedrooms. Ready
June 1. $125 + 10 for garage--$135. 2 year lease. 2
months in advance. Refrigerator, 6'; gas kitchen stove, 4
burner, 42"; steam heat--all furnished. Storage space and
washing machine in basement. Our choice appears to be D-4.
Living room window looks South on front court. Kitchen,
small bedroom, bath, each have 1 window on North. 1 large
bedroom has 1 window North, 1 West. 1 large Bedroom has
1 window West. Nice views West overlooking very large yard.
Living room radiator is under front window. 6 or 7 small
closets.

Application made April 14, dated April 13, for D-4,
with check for $125. 00. Roetta Building Corporation, 17
Maple Drive, Great Neck, Room 201, Great Neck 2418 and
6010. Lettering on window reads: Henry Laurence Corp.,
Consulting Mechanical Engineers.

May 16, 1948

Sunday, 16 May. Our 38th wedding anniversary!
Here we are at Great Neck and U.N.

Apartment. We leased Apartment D-4 and garage,
at 800 Middle Neck Road, for 28? months, at $135. And
we have paid 3 months in advance. Supposed to be ready
by June 1, but they won't be. We stayed in Colony House
Hotel--at $7.50 per for about 12 days.

House at 15 Brown Road. We have taken this furnished house at $225 per month for 2 months, from the
Henri Mindens. Moved in 14 May.

Margery will probably close the Evanston house around
June 1, and ship the furniture and Taffy [the family dog] and
come on by train.

Director of Division of Library Services of U.N. I'm
on the payroll from May 1. Actually reported at the office
May 4. Dorothy Compton is my secretary and good. Now
I've completed 2d week, 9 working days, plus a lot of home
work. And I've learned and done a lot.

Reorganization. Will become effective 17 May, after
announcement at staff meeting. The plan was evolved after
many discussions with library staff, Department of Public
Information chiefs, Moltu, Van Wijk, Osborne and others.
I'm sure as I can be about Reitman and [Violet A.] Cabeen
[head, Acquisitions Unit, and acting chief of Processing],
taking some chance on [Signe] Christensen [chief, Cataloging
Unit]. Perry is going to be unhappy.

Budget. We prepared additional justitications in a
report prepared for [William B.] Mumford [director, Division
of Special Services, Department of Public Information], for
the Secretary-General's annual report and other purposes;

a special memo for Cohen; talked at length with Van Wijk,
several times with Janecek, etc.   It looks now as if we
might get: a clerical pool of 9, a Deputy at $8200, an
executive assistant, 2 professional posts, a book and equipment fund of $108,000.   But there are more hurdles ahead.
More justifications are being prepared.

Letter to Library Committee.   First one written.
Goes out tomorrow.

Geneva.   Long letter sent to Breycha Friday with
Cohen's approval.   It asks a lot of questions which may
bring answers which will enable us to deal with the $64.00
question--what should be the role of Geneva Library?

Directors Meetings.   I have attended 2.   Not very important for me yet.   They occur every Tuesday.

Library Staff Meeting.   Have had one of all staff at
5:40 p.m. Cohen came late.   I talked.   2d one tomorrow
at 7:45 a.m.   There have been many small ones.   We shall
probably hold a weekly meeting of Chiefs of Sections and
Units--now reduced to 6.

. . .

Staff Committees.   Mrs. Cabeen and Miss Christensen
are working up a list of priorities.   Miss [Marie] Carroll
[reference librarian] heads a committee to prepare a list of
subjects of permanent interest.   [A.D.] Roberts [librarian,
Service to Readers Unit] is organizing a committee to draft
a book selection policy and more or less to administer it.

Borba.   We are about to offer him Rasmussen's post
August 1, expecting him to move to Deputy post January 1.

Contractual Services.   Still in progress.   Must get
going.

. . .

International Library Committee.   Plans are in the

making.   Looks like July 10 meeting.

Invitations.   Nell and I attended cocktail party at Town
Hall, United Staff Association of New York public libraries 9
May.   I'm going to banquet at Waldorf June 20 in honor of
Paul G. Hoffman [chairman, Board of Trustees, Committee
for Economic Development, and President, Studebaker Corp.].
To Boston with Nell for broadcast June 6.   To A. L. A.   June
13.   To tea at Brooklyn May 21.   To Chautauqua in August.
Am invited to A. L. A. Williamstown, June 26 or 27.   Am
invited to Maryland in October.

day.
      People.   Mrs. Roosevelt lunches at U.N. almost every

      . . .

Financial arrangements as they look now[20]

      . . .

May 22, 1948

      Another week.   Important events were:

      Banquet for Paul Hoffman given by C. E. D.   [Commit-
tee for Economic Development] at Waldorf.   Was glad to see:
Anne O'Hare McCormick [writer], Bill Benton [assistant
secretary of state], Marian Manley [business branch librarian,
Newark Public Library], Scotty Fletcher [Encyclopaedia Bri-
tannica Films], Chancellor [Harry W.] Chase [New York Uni-
versity], Beardsley Ruml [chairman of the board, R. H.
Macy and Co.], and to sit in the same room with Bernard
Baruch.

      Reception, 4-6, Brooklyn Public Library, for which
we arrived 1 hour and 20 minutes late, after several distinguished people--Rice, Bromfield [probably Louis, the au-
thor]--had gone.   Reasons: U.N. Library budget, Nell's
transportation by bus from Great Neck, my ignorance of how

to get there. Dinner at a club with Mr. [Milton J., chief librarian, Brooklyn Public Library] and Mrs. and Ruth Ferguson. Home by a better route.

At U.N., this was week assigned (by me) for personnel. U.N. calls it "contracts." After a 3 or 4 hour conference, we came out with unanimous recommendations. Involved were Reitman, Cabeen, Naprstek, [Moira] Figgis [acting chief, Research Section], [Harry N.M.] Winton [chief, Document Indexing Unit], Osborne.

. . .

Gossip. Word came to me that conversations in Janecek's office are reported and discussed by library staff before I have reported them even to Reitman and Cabeen. Damn! I think I'd better warn George Janecek to stop up the leaks.

Letter to Library Committee. Took a week to get it out, thanks to slowness of the mimeographing unit. Damn again.

May 31, 1948

As I look back over the first month, I recall:

The reorganization with Mrs. Cabeen and Reitman coming to top; the deplorable shortage of clerks, for the correction of which I'm sending a fairly strong memo to Cohen tomorrow. Copy will go also to Van Wijk; requests for reports for first one thing and then another; budget statements, on my own initiative or on request. I've got them all assembled now in a document sent to Van Wijk, dated 23 May. Miss Compton's efficiency and officiousness. Planning for the International Library Committee of Experts.

June 10-18, 1948

S. L. A. and A. L. A.   Went down to Washington for business (last) session of S. L. A.   Visited Sweetser's office in his absence.   Mostly worked or rested in my room. Wrote rather lengthy memo on internships, with Bob Lester in mind.

Went to Atlantic City, Hotel Dennis, Saturday p. m. Loafed Saturday night and Sunday.   Nell joined me Monday. We were showered with hospitality, gifts, and kindness. Were permitted to buy our own tickets to New Members dinner, but were guests at Newbery-Caldecott affair, Friends of Libraries and perhaps others.

Executive Board gave us a small dinner Wednesday evening.   Presented Nell with a check for $30. 00 for a present to be purchased by her.

Gave me a Wonder-rod by Shakespeare and a dozen or 13 flies plus a line, plus a check for $25. 50.   I shall probably use the last for waders and a reel. [21]

Quite a party!

I made a little speech at the Friends Luncheon.

Thursday was one Big Day, at the General Session.

1st the Lippincott Award for me and a dozen red roses for Nell.

Then speeches about me by Ralph Munn [director, Carnegie Library, Pittsburgh], Harry Lydenberg [director, A. L. A. International Relations Office, Washington--see Appendix D][22] (read by [Milton E.] Lord [director, Boston Public Library]), and Robbie [E. S. Robinson, librarian, Vancouver Public Library].   And I replied, making the same little speech I had made the day before.

Not knowing about the award, we were waiting behind

the curtain and we came in very dramatically in spite of our-
selves when Joe [Joseph W. Lippincott, donor of the award]
asked "Where's Carl Milam?" Audience stood twice to greet
us!

June 22, 1948

Two or 3 things happened today.

Dr. [O.] Frey [chief of section] (Judge?) of the Security
Council, Atomic Energy group, to tell me about an Atomic
Energy bibliography in preparation, asked some cooperation.
I liked him.

. . .

I joined W. Martin Hill [deputy executive assistant and
director for coordination of Specialized Agencies and Economic
and Social Matters] and Dr. [Szeming] Sze [chief of Specialized
Agencies Section] in preparation of my first "Paper"--an E
document on proposed transfer of Health libraries in Geneva
Library to WHO. It opposes the transfer now.

Gjesdal had a call from Molitiev (?)--not Molotov--
Assistant to [Andrei A.] Gromyko [Soviet permanent representative to the U.N.]--expressing interest in International
Committee of Library Experts and asking for copy of agenda
which had been left out of his letter.

[Louis J.] Bailey [chief librarian, Queens Borough
Public Library] and [Charles H.] Compton [librarian, St.
Louis Public Library] came for a visit.[23]   Mrs. Cabeen
lunched with us.

July 28, 1948[24]

. . .

October 27, 1948[25]

. . .

October 28, 1948

My poor neglected diary: I may or will give up any thought of keeping a real diary but I hope I can persuade myself to make a list of some important events, and both a list and a file of important memos.

Some of these events and memos are noted here from memory, and ought to be revised. The file should be started forthwith.

Early conferences and memos. See first part of this book.

Rasmussen.

Clerical pool.

Budget preparation and justifications. April, May, June.

Staff reorganization

Appointment of Rubens Borba de Moraes.

Appointment, and meeting International Advisory Committee of Library Experts. Working papers. Report.

Internship project.

Contractual arrangements.

Spending our book and binding money.

European trip. General report and Geneva Library report.

Some Future Jobs. Action on reports of European trip. Exchanges. Branch of Geneva Library.

Policy for Secretary General and 5th Committee.

Select new appointees. Get them at once.

Weekly index to U.N. and Specialized Agency Documents. Stavridi and Van Wijk will support.

Building planning.

1950 Budget.

Letter to Library Committee.

Letter to International Advisory Committee of Library Experts about reception of the report, and use of it for policy statement.

November 28, 1948

This is not a very consistent diary.

How did the Big Shots who have kept diaries ever manage to do it?

Or did they? Maybe they mostly kept personal copies of all correspondence, memos, etc. arranged chronologically. In my case that would cover most of it, but not all.

For example: there is nothing in the file--I do not keep personal copies--to report:

During the Budget Committee hearing in Paris about 20 October 1948, Trygvie Lie came to the top table and sat in the 2d row alongside me. Transfer of Library to Department of Public Information and possible--quite impossible actually--shape of the Geneva Library were being criticized. Proposal was made by Holland that Library be given a semi-independent status under the Secretary General.

"My God, I don't want it," said the S.G.

Somewhat later, a remark was (unfortunately) made by Miss [Beatrice] Howell [a World Health Organization representative to the U.N.] of WHO indicating that the Geneva Library was about to transfer some materials to WHO for indefinite loan. "Is that so?" asked the Secretary General. I handed him the draft of the proposal and he nodded approval. Miss Howell was right but had given a wrong impression.

Nor would I find in any file a document reporting:

(1) That on Tuesday 3 November at a staff meeting to discuss personnel problems--Miss Osborne and Miss [Claire] Howe

[Appointments and Staff Relations Division, Bureau of Personnel] present--I asked them how in Hell we were expected to get on with our job of providing library service when for 4 months we had been prevented from filling a vacancy in the Trusteeship Departmental Library by Personnel Regulations. We had come up with 6 or 8 candidates, all competent, and all had been turned down for geographical or other reasons. One was Norwegian; Trygvie Lie vetoed even temporary appointment. Another was a sister-in-law of a member of the Secretariat; no go.

Another, Miss Rona [liaison librarian, Department of Trusteeship and Non-Self-Governing Territories], had been appointed, but release from another Department was denied because she was irreplaceable. (We were not offering her a promotion, but she wished to come.)

Now Miss Rona was available; why not move at once? Next day I called Miss Osborne. She wanted to be sure Miss Rona really had the qualifications. I blew up and said I could not work with anybody who made a decision one week and wanted to act the following week as if we were starting from scratch. Personnel had approved Rona six weeks ago; do we have to start all over again now? Miss Osborne concurred under pressure.

Reitman reported at once to Mrs. Frost [probably a secretary or administrative assistant] in Janecek's office. Her [Rona's] transfer was to be made almost immediately.

In the afternoon--just as a necessary precaution, -- I dropped in on Mrs. Frost. No, Mr. Janecek had raised some question. I called George out of a meeting and asked what the Hell. Well, Mrs. Frost had told him that Reitman had told her that Personnel had previously decided Rona was not qualified. He (Janecek) and I called Personnel asking why they were now willing to appoint her, unqualified, instead of a Miss Geddes, a sister-in-law. So I blew up again--after four months of frustration--and asked George why he had to stick his oar in. I was fed up with being paid about $1000 a month (gross) to do a job and being prevented by red tape from doing it.

Actually of course, in the light of what Reitman was reported to have said--but actually had not said--Janecek was right, or more or less so. I apologized, and he instructed Mrs. Frost to go ahead.

Presumably Miss Rona will be on the job 29 November ber!!!

Another unrecorded incident is that Byron Price asked me in Paris where in the Secretariat the Library Services should be. I told him privately that I doubted the appropriateness of being in the Department of Public Information, but that, if asked the question publicly, I would answer that so far as I can see it makes little difference as long as the library is permitted and aided to render an organization-wide service without favors to the Department in which we are, that Department of Public Information has facilitated this kind of service and has asked for no special favors.

Mr. Price later stated to the Budget Committee he had recommended to the Secretary General that the Library be directly under him but that so far the Secretary General had not seen fit to approve the suggestion.

December 31, 1948

This should be an appropriate time to set down a few additional items which should have been recorded as they occurred.

But I did not do it.

January 8, 1949

8 months have gone. The letter of 1 January to the Library Committee [see Appendix E] reports some progress and predicts some things to come.[26]

Biggest recent event is the trial run of a Weekly Index to documents, and an effort to get it going on a permanent basis. We think we can get out two issues, and that these two may make continuation inevitable. Cohen and Janecek promise full and vigorous support.

Helen Wessells is about to complete a listing of U.N. research activities and other jobs which have implications for library service, which may form the basis for our Policy statement.[27]

I hope to insert here a short listing [of] problems and activities ahead; also the 1 January letter of which we issued 1000 copies.

January 9, 1949

Work Ahead.

(1a) Continuous. Policy statement--CHM. Budget 1950--All chiefs of sections and units. Building planning-- Moraes. (1b) For January. More reading room space-- E. Reitman. Annual leave schedule--Gomez [Guido Gomez de Silva, research assistant and assistant to Milam]. Review contractual services--Reitman and Moraes. Personnel vacancies--Moraes. Weekly Index--Reitman and CHM. Survey Documents Indexing Unit--CHM. Woodrow Wilson Library-- CHM. WHO--CHM. Research Section--CHM. Opinion Survey Section--CHM. Section Meeting, Processing--Moraes. Shaw, arrears, reclassification--Moraes. I.A.C.L.E. report --Moraes. List of periodical articles--Reitman.

(2) Soon as possible. Contracts foreign libraries--CHM.

Library Committee meeting. Staff meetings. Action European report. Review book selection policy. Specialized Agency documents distribution--Reitman. Assembly Library, Flushing. (3) <u>Keep in mind</u>. Bibliographies. Depositories. Departmental Libraries--more staff. Interns and exchanges. Geneva improvements. Sorting, selecting, discarding. Acquisition lists. Map unit survey. Transfer Document Indexing to Processing? Service to Information Centers.

<u>April 7, 1949</u>

Since the 1 January letter--which has had a very good reception--

Two meetings of our Library Committee; the first filled with praise and constructive criticism; the second endorsed preparations for moving. That endorsement, probably more than anything else, may win us our 38 1949 and 25 or 27 1950 new posts.

Other steps included special memos to Gjesdal, with copies to Price and Martin Hill. Both invited me to their offices for talks, which were most encouraging.

Moraes resigns. Damn. Who next.

Gietz not available now for Service to Readers Chief.

[Dr. James T.] Shotwell [of the Carnegie Endowment for International Peace] conference. [28]

Raymond Fosdick conference coming next week.

Policy statement pressing. And a lot more.

Nell and Margery both ill!

And I need a vacation.

Interpretation wants Gomez.

<u>April 21, 1949</u>

This may prove to be an important day for me in U.N.

[Victor] da Silva [administrative officer, Budget Division Bureau of Finance] says he will recommend--apropos my policy and organization statement--that Library be transferred to Secretary-General's office, and asking what should be in the Library when transferred. Should it include: Research Section? Opinion Survey? Language Reference Center? Archives?

Byron Price and Bruce Turner [executive officer, Department of Administrative and Financial Services] had already anticipated the recommendation. In fact Price told me and told the Fifth Committee in Paris last October that he had previously made this recommendation.

This sort of puts me on the spot with Department of Public Information.

My official position is one of neutrality. I have suffered from being in D.P.I. [Department of Public Information] in only one way. That is budget-wise. Advisory Committee and 5th Committee are very hard on Cohen and D.P.I. and while Library is in D.P.I. we must take some of the punishment. But Cohen is helpful and friendly and likes to help the Library. He has not interfered in operations. He might if the Director didn't know his own mind.

July 1, 1949

Budget hearing before Advisory Committee in June not too bad. [N.] Sundarasan [member, Advisory Committee on Administrative and Budgetary Questions] thought I ought to tell Secretary-General that some subjects were not appropriate for investigation by U.N.!

We are set up as independent agency in Secretary-General's office--in Budget. Cordier has spoken about it and I have sent him material. In my memo I mentioned job of finding my successor after next April 30.

Rubens is gone. [Andrew D.] Osborn [assistant librarian, Harvard University Library] arrived today for 3
months, thank God.

[Willard] Heaps [chief, Service to Readers Unit] arrived 15 June and is doing a fine job.

Finding their successors is my big task.[29] Also a
successor to Miss Christensen.

"Preparations for Moving" has been a success so far.
We have a flock of temporary assistants on the job or coming.
12 + 22 + whatever indexers we get.

Policy statement is out of the way.

Organization statement (as if from A.F.S. [Department
of Administrative and Financial Services]) also.

da Silva has been a great, a very great, help to us in
budget, organization and temporary help.

It is now rumored that we may not move to Manhattan
until the middle of 1957.

My office is still in a mess but Miss [Janet] West
[secretary], Miss Byron [clerk-stenographer] and Guido
[Gomez de Silva] (when not on home leave) are working very
hard.

We have apparently failed to get the Woodrow Wilson
Library. Anti-government, Princeton, academic combine
against governmental organization--so I am informally told.

Building planning takes a lot of time.

Big problem to get U.S.S.R. librarians.

Too many newspapers?

For budget hearing we prepared special memos or
figures on: Cost of binding, administrative assistant 9 to administrative officer 11 (Gomez), book selection and buying

procedures, acquisition costs, cataloging costs, contractual
services, departmental libraries, newspapers, magazines,
U.S.S.R. acquisitions.   We are getting Conference Room 14
for fireproof storage.

July 6, 1949

Heard yesterday Secretary General has called upon
Department of Public Information to find posts for 5 grade
13's selected by certain under-represented delegations; that
it is rumored the Secretariat must absorb 20 or more such
political choices.   What's all the talk about building up an
international civil service?

We are trying to get 22 temporary posts.   Was told
2 weeks ago we would get them.   We are all set with people
for several posts.   But the authorization doesn't come through.

Have just talked with M. Noel Monod, Treasury Section, who told me more than I wanted to know about invest-
ments.   But I was pleased to learn that the Library Endowment Fund (Geneva)[30] is over $535,000.   Displeased to learn
that some $75,000 Greek and German investments are worth-
less.   Pleased that policy is now to invest more in U.S. and
Canada, but some in Switzerland.

July 10, 1949

On the 8th, the only 2 trained Siamese librarians in
existence were introduced to each other by CHM in the U.N.
Headquarters Library: [Chun] Prabha, trained in Manila and
Ann Arbor, who is working with his delegation and broadcasting for Department of Public Information in Siamese, who
wishes to devote his life to the development of libraries in
his country; and Miss [Rabieb] Tantranon who has had a couple
of years at Illinois, and is working for our Library on a
Carnegie Endowment internship.

There is less pressure on me now than at any time since 1 January. If I had Osborn and Heaps permanently I could relax. [René Ferdinand Malan] Immelman [librarian, University of Cape Town] is a little bit interested in the Moraes job but asks no decision until he arrives late August. Appointment should be as of 1 October. Gietz has not answered. I should get more inquiries out.

A Book about U.N. I've been wondering lately if I could write a book about the U.N. which would be useful and maybe bring in a small income. To do the latter it should be a school or college textbook, or something approaching that.

So far my thoughts have taken these two forms:

1. A book divided into 3 parts:

    a. Political

    b. Economic

    c. Social

Meaning the ways in which the U.N. contributes to maintenance of peace, or at least, international understanding, through activities in these categories.

2. A 4th part which would set up a plan for the organization of a U.N. within the school or college, with General Assembly, Security Council, ECOSOC, etc.

I don't know enough, but maybe I could learn if I worked at it.

Of course there would be a bibliography.

O.K., it's an idea worth playing with. See pages at end of this book under U.N. [31]

July 19, 1949

Yesterday Byron Price called me in to report Advisory Committee action on my Budget. Cuts of $24,400 proposed.

$4,400 for contractual services. $20,000 for Manning Table, mentioning Departmental Libraries additional staff and 1 clerk to recover overdue books.   I presented my arguments in a memo.   Suggested yielding 1st on contracts, account and loan desk clerk, and last on departmental assistants.

Osborn, Heaps and [Dorothy M.] Drake [librarian, Department of Social Affairs] are doing a fine job.

We have recently hired 9 catalogers and 9 clerks for Osborn and 4 or 5 temporaries, including Drake, for Departmental Libraries.   For 4 months.   How do we keep them 6?

August 31, 1949

Last question is answered.   After my 4-memo attack, Personnel capitulated on most points.   We can reappoint any we wish for balance of year.   That is wonderful and I wrote a memo to [Georges] Palthey [director, Bureau of Personnel] saying so.

Then yesterday Bob Hausner [chief, Administrative Placement Section, Appointments and Staff Relations Division] said there really was no such discrimination against foreign clerks hired in New York as he had previously said.   But after a reasonable Chapter 13 appointment,[32] they must com-pete with regulars on the register.   We are permitted to have Danino for 2 more months.

Mrs. Cabeen spoke in praise of Heaps yesterday, hav-ing finally been won over.

Jerome K. Wilcox is with us for 1 month.   Setting up procedures for card indexing of documents.   Hope to keep him on as consultant for 4 or 5 months.

Winton, after our serious talk, is troublesome.   But he has put [Hugo] Knoepfmacher [index analyst] in charge of binding project.   Caballero [i.e., Fernando Caballero-

Marsal, index analyst] is being given increasing responsibility.
So, maybe we are on the way.

Book fund in bad shape. Discussed with da Silva.
He gave back to us the $6500 we had offered to release.
Wonderful!

Then yesterday he informed me through Guido that
Mr. Price wanted Library to be sure to spend all of its money
this year. That may mean $10,000-$16,000 more we can
spend for temporary help this year. And that means something like 14 clerks or more for 3 1/2 months. Hot dog!
We know how to use it and them. Space for more people is
becoming a problem.

Osborn's post. No prospect. Gietz has not answered.
Immelman has been in U.S. for maybe 2 weeks without getting
in touch with me. Gosh!

Chief of Catalog Unit. [Wen-Yu] Yen [cataloger] is best
bet. But doubt if he is ready for it. Maybe so if I can keep
Osborn on as consultant. Must consult Osborn and [Keyes D.]
Metcalf [director, Harvard University Library]--at once.

Coordinating Library Committee. Meeting in Geneva
of European members. Reitman presiding.

Advisory Committee. Proposes cuts of $24,900, less
than 5 (or is it 4) %. Price opposes most of these cuts on
my advice. I'm fighting to retain $17,000 for new depart-
mental library assistants.

Dinner at da Silvas. Mr. and Mrs. Eriksen, Mr. [A.
Dardeau, chief, Technical and General Placement Section,
Appointments and Staff Relations Division] and Mrs. Vieira,
Mr. [H.A., chief, Territorial Research and Analysis Section]
and Mrs. Wieschhoff and others. Late August.

New publications. Recent accessions, starts 1 September, monthly. Selected articles in periodicals--occasional.

Latin American Bibliography.   Library leaflet--invitation to
use library.   Bibliography of Specialized Agencies.
    I thought we were off to a good start in 1948.   Maybe
so.   But what progress we are making in 1949!
    Wonder if I'll retire next May 1?
    Nell and I have discovered polo.

December 6, 1949

    I am the world's worst diarist.
    Returning from vacation in Illinois and Indiana, I find:
Reitman et al. have done a good job.
    They have chosen people from among our temporaries
for permanent posts, satisfactorily on the whole.   But they
had used all of our temporary funds, or nearly.   Yesterday
in conference and with complete unanimity--God Bless Em--
we reserved $7000 for later allocation.
    Guido had impressed Edouard as being a man of great
ability, likely to be director of this Library in 15 years.
    Janet West appears to him to be a good receptionist
but 1st class all-around secretary.
    da Silva is a very valuable ally.   We were short of
equipment funds; he arranged a transfer--at once--from our
Book Fund, with Tilney.   And is helpful in a hundred ways.
But maybe not on the highest level.
    Yesterday I ran into Martin Hill.   Swell guy.   He
greeted me warmly.   Wondered how we would handle administrative matters when Library goes over to Secretary-General's
office.   I said Cordier had remarked he didn't want to be
bothered; that Budget referred to Library as an independent
office; that we were hoping for a meeting with [David] Blickenstaff [executive officer and chief, General Assembly Affairs
and Administrative Section]; that I wanted to handle our affairs

in line with Executive Office policy but without bothering that office; thought we could deal directly with Budget and Personnel. He expressed complete agreement and suggested that he and Cordier be invited to the meeting. I have reported this to da Silva, Reitman and Gomez.

But there are some serious problems.

The Grade 16 post--Chief of Processing--is still hanging fire. Palthey will argue for Gietz, I for Immelman.

Grade 12, Chief of Cataloging Unit, Yen, [Jorgen K.] Nielsen [cataloger], Krikana. All good but not sufficiently experienced. Should have Miss [Susan] Haskins [chief, Catalog Unit, on loan from Harvard University] or Isabel [la] Rhodes [retired from Columbia University Library] or other strong person 6 months or year longer. Osborn will ask Metcalf about Haskins.

Willard Heaps is not yet confirmed beyond 31 December. We hope to keep him.

Personnel will insist on considering "redundant" clerks to whom U.N. has a long-standing obligation instead of clerks experienced in our own shop.

Consultant fees to Osborn and Wilcox have large assessments against them which seem to me unfair. Osborn is paying $40 to $50 out of his own pocket for each trip because no per diem is allowed.

I have been asked to stay another year beyond 30 April. Shall I accept? (1) Nell's health? (2) My own? (3) How much can I save? (4) Shall I be hamstrung by Personnel?

In 1950-51 I should be able to save:

Annuity 185 x 12	$2,220
Annuity payments 12 x 150	1,800
Salary above 1000	1,000
	5,020

Annuity payment from U.N. is $40 per month, and salary increase should be verified.

(5) Successor. Will U.N. be willing to double encumber my post for 6 months before I leave? Unless Reitman is chosen?

. . .

December 29, 1959[33]

Here are answers (as of 29 December) to questions on previous page:

1. Up and down. What effect this environment is having on it I can't figure out. None as far as I can see, but how can I know?

2. My medical exam reveals nothing bad. Urine, blood, heart, chest x-ray, blood pressure--O. K. Dr. says I should reduce to 180 and exercise lightly.

3. About $5000. Maybe $6000 in 18 months.

4. I am. Can I win out? Is it worth the struggle? See below--29 December.

5. My guess is yes.

Items 1 and 4 are still serious questions.

December 15, 1949

I have just come from a talk with Byron Price about Gietz vs. Immelman. He didn't and won't let me down.

It is quite a long story which I should like to put in the record here if I don't sneeze too much.

First, Mr. Price.

He asked about vacation. We talked about trees and farms. He has a place near Aurora. Was born in northern Indiana. (I forgot to express the hope that he wouldn't leave the U.N. for a post in the State Department.) It had been solidly wooded with black walnut--one stump 8 feet in diameter,

beautiful curly wood. All trees had been cut and burned so
corn could be grown. His father had later planted one acre
of walnut seed.

I thanked him for the offer of another year. Said I
had not accepted until after medical examination. He said
he was surprised to learn I was 65, I was so active. Thank
you. He hoped I would stay. He had been surprised to
learn my 2 years would be up April 30, 1950.

I said I was glad he had had a chance to talk with
Reitman, that everything had gone smoothly under his leader-
ship in my absence.

Then I barged into the Gietz-Immelman case, with
regret that I had to bring it to him, as I thought Directors
should settle these matters themselves. His reply was "That
is what I am here for."

I told him:

That the position has been vacant since early June
except for Osborn's 3 months;

That I had recruited actively and extensively in South
America, South Africa and Sweden, having been told they were
under-represented countries; that I had found no one of the
right calibre in Sweden, Immelman, the leading librarian in
South Africa, and had suggested to Palthey a few names in
Argentina;

That Immelman was obviously the best and was so
recognized by Palthey;

That 2 Argentinians had eliminated themselves;

. . .

That we--Palthey and I--had proposed a special post
as bibliographer after I had refused to accept Gietz as chief
of processing even temporarily;

That Bureau of Budget had turned this down;

That I had said we could not afford it out of our appropriation;

That Bureau of Budget had said also it was wrong in principle to create a post to satisfy international recruiting requirements;

That this was one of the two top posts under the Director of the Library and that we could not risk the danger of loss of esprit de corps--which is now excellent--by taking someone in an administrative post who does not work well with his associates;

That I was not averse to giving national preference in lower positions;

And probably a good deal more--but that I could not accept Gietz as chief of processing.

Price was sympathetic.

He would take a similar stand if he were in my place.

He supposed Palthey was in great pressure from the Argentine delegation.

I said I was willing to take him as a bibliographer without administrative responsibility.

Mentioned the need for a bibliographer, especially in connection with Technical Assistance; that Gietz is an experienced bibliographer and educated in the natural sciences, in which the Library staff is weak; that Technical Assistance has large funds for unassigned purposes.

Price said Palthey was next on his schedule and he was glad I had reported my trouble.

Finally, I hoped he would help me out; and his answer was "I will arrange something."

Meantime Price had said that if Delegations insisted on international representation, they should expect to pay for it. Implication was that some funds should be made available

--in addition to administrative needs--for extra people to provide representatives of under-represented countries.

Supplementary notes, if any further remarks are recalled:[34]

Now for some recent history:

In September and October we had interviewed Immelman. My associates--Osborn, Reitman, Heaps and Cabeen--joined in recommending him. So also did Howe, Osborne and Hausner of Personnel.

Immelman was interested. Later (in November) he withdrew his name because of the attitude of his University. The latter was not reported to Personnel because I still hoped to get him. Idea was and is to have Price and U.N. Mission cable to University.

I went on November vacation saying his appointment could be put through in my absence, but no other for that post.

Reitman wrote action was stalled; more consideration must be given to Gietz and also that Immelman had withdrawn his application but that this had not been reported to Personnel.

On my return I learned that Hausner wished to arrange a talk between me and Palthey. It was finally scheduled around the 9th of December.

Conference of Palthey, Hausner and Milam.

We talked about trees and shrubs, U.S.A. and France. Then we came to the subject.

I had copies of a parallel column statement on Gietz and Immelman, prepared by Gomez and one was handed to Palthey. He pushed it aside almost without a glance, saying Immelman was obviously the better candidate but we must have an Argentine citizen in a high post.

I explained or stated that dissension had existed in the Library staff when I came; that we are now a very smooth working team; that the team worked smoothly and effectively under Reitman in my absence; that I could not take a chance of wrecking this machine by bringing in a man who doesn't get on well with staff or other associates.

I reminded him that during the 6 months plus vacancy (except for Osborn 3 months) I had recruited vigorously in the underrepresented areas of Latin America, Sweden and South Africa; that I had given him several names for investigation in Latin America; that I had wanted Gietz, a personal friend, but that the comments about him made him unacceptable for Chief of Processing.

Palthey asked about my future plans. I answered about _my_ future. But he was thinking about my successor.

I said I did not agree with Moraes in principle that it must be an American but that it certainly should be a competent library administrator in the modern sense. I think I mentioned Francis and Clapp, and Reitman, repeating that Reitman had done a swell job as Acting Director in November.

He thought we might bring Immelman in later and consider him. From what happened later I suspect he was thinking also, and more, of Gietz as a candidate for that post.

(My conviction at this moment is that Francis and Clapp are out because of geography; that the U.N. would profit most if I could get Immelman here soon, give him and Reitman each every possible chance to show their capabilities --and let the best man win. I am sure Reitman would do a good job and I suspect that Immelman would too but can't be sure.)

I was urged to take Gietz on a temporary job. I said O.K. if on a special assignment, but not as Chief of Processing

even for 3 months.   I could squeeze 3 months salary out of
our temporary assistance funds, but no more.

At one time Palthey suggested that we get both on a
temporary basis, but that was discarded.

I said we might have waited too long to get Immelman
but Palthey spoke of cabling the University and was sure we
could get him.

Finally it was agreed that we would ask Bureau of
Finance to create a new post of chief bibliographer, grade
16, and offer it to Gietz and that we would offer Chief of
Processing, 16, to Immelman.   I had agreed to a similar
proposal when it was made by Hausner 2 months before.
(As I left Palthey asked if we could use a Uruguayan and I
said yes.   Piniero at a 9 or 10 when we had a vacancy.)

Hausner said this was a "package" and that I should
not communicate with Immelman until Bureau of Finance had
acted.   He would see [Laurence] Michelmore [chief, Budget
Division] Monday morning.

I was at home with a cold Monday and Tuesday.

Victor da Silva called up saying matter was in his
hands.   Asked whether I could divert from our budget enough
for the new post and I said no.   Maximum was three months
from our money.   He indicated lack of sympathy with Palthey's
proposal.

On Wednesday I was told that Bureau of Finance had
said no.

On Thursday morning I was informed by Hausner that
Palthey insisted that Gietz be appointed as Chief of Processing.   I refused.   He said I might see Price and Lie, and indicated that sometimes orders came down from Lie and could
not be refused.

Reitman, Cabeen, Heaps and Gomez were in my office

and I reported to them, suggesting in my disgust that I might
be farming next spring instead of a year later.

Mrs. Cabeen indicated she might be looking for a job
in New York. Reitman suggested negotiations, mentioning
again our real need for a bibliographer and Gietz's obvious
qualifications in bibliography and science. Mrs. Cabeen was
even willing to give up one grade 16 post and get along without a Chief of Processing for a time. Reitman opposed this.
Reitman urged me not to take an uncompromising attitude.
I insisted it was not just personal offense at not getting my
way, but that in principle I was convinced that patronage
could wreck the U.N. Someone suggested that I accept under
protest, but it was quickly agreed that that would serve no
useful purpose. I agreed not to oppose Gietz as a bibliographer but thought I must continue to refuse to accept him as
Chief of Processing.

Meantime I had got an appointment with Price for
3 p.m.

I saw da Silva and got a full report from him. Later
he read it to me over the telephone.

He said the Bureau of Finance and the Bureau of Personnel would back me in my position.

Miss Osborne wished me luck and hoped I would tell
her all about my interview.

I talked briefly with da Silva on the telephone, but
Miss Osborne was out.

December 16, 1949

Miss Osborne reported that Price advised Palthey to
go to work on the Budget Bureau again. If people must be
taken for geographical reasons the money for them must be
found.

Bob Hausner said we could probably fill both jobs early the following week.

Miss Julia Henderson [chief, Policy Division, Bureau of Finance] and Miss ...[35] came to discuss an S.G.B. [Secretary-General's Bulletin] transferring Library to the Executive Office. Hausner and da Silva were present. Everybody agreed Library should be treated as an independent agency. Blickenstaff was reported to have the same opinion.

December 29, 1949

The Personnel Bureau is making my life miserable, consuming most of my time, hampering seriously the work of the Library, forcing us to do things which are obviously wrong, promoting inefficiency and extravagance.

It would take more time than I wish to give to set down the whole story but here are some items:

Immelman-Gietz story already told. Still not finished. I suspect that I am being persecuted somewhat because of my refusal to accept Gietz except in a new post.

Jacobsen [temporary library staff member]. Hausner will not approve a 3-months' extension of a Chapter 13 (temporary) but would approve 6 months. Promotion impossible because here too short a time.

Berlant [temporary library staff member]. Wanted from month to month to fill Munzer [acquisitions librarian] vacancy because of illness. No, because he has been here 4 months on Chapter 13!

Miss [Enid Maria] Baa [senior cataloger]? I wanted her for 3 months out of temporary assistance funds. No. Chapter 13 again. So I'm forced to take her for 6, costing U.N. about $750 because of a regulation.

[Surjit] Singh. Here first as intern. Later as

temporary employee at grade 7. We want him for 1 year at grade 8. Oh no. Can't possibly promote after so short a time. He wants his wife brought over. So Claire Howe is trying: (1) to get him as a new recruit at 8 and to give him (with my approval) a 2 year contract so he can get his wife over.

What is the status of these troublesome regulations? They are not in the Manual. Victor da Silva has never seen them. We have not seen them. Do they exist? Have they any authority? Has Price ever seen and approved them?

In my present opinion the Personnel Bureau is in about the same condition as the Library was when I came, namely, chaotic. I could write a book telling why.

. . .

Three or four other redundant clerks are being forced down our throats although they appear to be duds.

What Reitman calls the Personnel Bureau's "omnibus" corruption of categories is part of the trouble. There appears to be an unwillingness to consider any special qualifications required in a particular grade 3 post. The Personnel Bureau's idea is that any average grade 3 can do any grade 3 job. We know that is not so. A generally good grade 3 might be unable to make good letters and figures on the backs of books. A big husky grade 3 or 4 who would be fine at heaving boxes is not necessarily adept at filing cards or pamphlets.

There is also a "wooden" unimaginative acceptance of ratings. Personnel Bureau makes no effort to ascertain by telephone or conversation why a redundant person was not kept or for what kind of work he is suited.

When we rated a man unfit for the rather specialized and somewhat finicky tasks he had been assigned to do in the

Library but added that he would be good for some other job
at the same grade, he was sacked by Personnel Bureau. Can
we ever get another honest rating?

The effect on our budget is bad because this forces on
us people with advanced steps and accrued vacation and home
leave.

. . .

December 31, 1949

Yesterday was quite a day. Several pleasant things
happened other than New Year's greetings.

. . .

Reitman got notice of his promotion from grade 15 to
16, which has been pending for at least one year.

Personnel Bureau decided it could appoint Singh for
one year to Grade 8 (now 7) and bring his wife to this
country.

Rockefeller Foundation decided to give [Jacdish] Sharma
[library intern] a 6-months' grand-in-aid so he can have more
experience with us.

We actually did get a check off to the Library of Congress out of contract funds in 1950 budget. Several people
helped, especially Guido. Bergh says it never happened before.

Guido's trial was postponed.

Blickenstaff of Executive Office of the Secretary-General said he would write a memo from Cordier to Price making me the certifying officer of Library which would make us
able to handle our own internal administrative problems.

We were encouraged to believe that our space problems
in Social Affairs may be solved.

About January 4, 1950

. . . 36

Topics on which I should write notes for this diary: More Immelman, Gietz. [David] Owen [assistant secretary-general, Department of Economic Affairs], Bob [probably Robert Hausner], Palthey. Haskins. Carnegie Endowment study. Woodrow Wilson [Memorial Library]. [Clyde] Eagleton [professor of international law, New York University], Sweetser. Assistant Secretary General Owen. Building re-modeling, moving. Re-evaluation of posts and people. December indexing.

January 6, 1950 or thereabouts.

I have just come from my first Promotion Board meeting--Palthey, [B.V.K.] Menon, Miss Howe and another (Mrs. Goldrick) from Personnel; [Sturgis] Shields [administrative officer, Department of Economic Affairs], [Finn] Munch-Petersen [chief, Administrative Section], and Gowans.

No objection on Haskins on assurance another renewal would not be requested; that Yen, Nielsen or Krikana would be proposed.

Palthey spoke against Heaps on geographical grounds, saying if we appoint him for a year, and he is as good as we say, he will not be fired for geographical reasons. It's therefore bad. He asked for opinions of Shields, Munch-Petersen, and Gowans. All said in effect: "What else can you do?" And Palthey yielded.

In the course of the discussion Palthey spoke of a South African as being in the post of Chief of Processing.

February 23, 1950

Immelman-Gietz. Reitman and I talked with [Francis

P.E.] Green, Executive Officer of Economic Affairs and his associate, Shields. Former appeared to think it would not be unreasonable to pay a bibliographer out of Technical Assistance funds. But, several days later Bob Hausner reported:

1. That Assistant Secretary-General Owen had vetoed the idea.

2. That Palthey had authorized posting the job and putting both names before the Senior Promotions Board.

And that's where we are now. Board meeting may be held most any day this week or next. Price will preside. I'll be present; also a Secretary-General or Top Ranking Director or two. Cordier said he would arrange to have his endorsement of Immelman known by somebody at that meeting. I still think I'll win.

Woodrow Wilson Library. Elsewhere in my U.N. material is a copy of my letter of 10 February to Cleveland E. Dodge [president, Woodrow Wilson Foundation]. It was suggested and largely drafted by Arthur Sweetser, though I put it in final shape, after approval by and some suggestions from Martin Hill, Abe Feller [general counsel and principal director, Legal Department], Hans Andersen [director, Bureau of Finance], Byron Price and finally the Secretary-General himself. Andersen said we could find the money outside the Library budget and decision may come at meeting 24 March.

Clyde Eagleton will be helpful, but if the U.N. gets that library, it is Arthur Sweetser who will deserve the credit.

U.N. Documents Index. First issue of this monthly appeared on 17 March.[37] I distributed several copies personally. It has been well received but has caused no sensation.

February 27, 1950

Mrs. [Julie] d'Estournelles [executive director,

Woodrow Wilson Foundation] called today to arrange for me to meet some of the directors of Woodrow Wilson Foundation soon at Manhattan Building.

Big jobs now are: Re-evaluation of posts--which will have the effect of upgrading professionals and lowering eventual salaries of clerks. Most of our senior professionals should be upgraded.

Budget for 1951. Sorry, but we must ask for more people to man new building in 1951.

Woodrow Wilson Library--personal calls. In danger of being neglected.

March 8, 1950

Made a brief talk tonight to Nassau Library Association on films.

Woodrow Wilson Foundation special committee meets with Reitman and me tomorrow late afternoon at Manhattan Building.

. . .

Immelman-Gietz. Senior promotion board set for next Monday.

Trygvie Lie reception at his home Friday 6-8.

Pat Blair [chief film library specialist, Film Project Office, A. L. A. , New York], Julien Bryan [International Film Foundation] and [Jan Gunnar] Lindstrom [deputy director, Films and Visual Information Division] (U.N. films) lunched with me today.

Paid my last installment on Metropolitan annuity today. Should receive first payment coming my way on 1 April.

Over past week-end Nell and I tentatively decided we would probably stay 6 months from 1 May. That is through 31 October. We should have about $9000 reserve by then. Final decision after next Monday's decision on Immelman. I want to take Nell South next winter--or maybe Southwest.

March 9, 1950

Immelman-Gietz. Bob Hausner reported that Bureau of Personnel will recommend Immelman at Senior Promotions Board meeting Monday morning!!! Wonderful. But what a pity we could not have reached this conclusion last October.

. . .

Woodrow Wilson Library. Reitman and I met a special committee at Manhattan Building last evening: [Frank] Altschul [director and secretary, Council on Foreign Relations], Mrs. [Agnes Brown] Leach [director, Foreign Policy Association], Sweetser and Eagleton. Also Mrs. d'Estournelles and Miss [Harriet] Van Wyck [librarian, Woodrow Wilson Memorial Library]. Also Mr. [Michael] Harris [of Harrison, Abramovitz and Harris] architect.

They asked questions about building, looked at plans and saw the 3d floor (present) which showed how spacious a reading room could be provided. I think they were impressed. Harriet Van Wyck, Ed Reitman and I did a good job. Many were impressed by the provision of study rooms.

March 13, 1950

The Immelman case was closed today, my way. Now we must get him!

My first Senior Promotions Board. It makes me think librarians are pretty undergraded.

Woodrow Wilson Library situation looks pretty good. Telephone calls from Julie d'Estournelles and Sweetser. Must finish my letter tomorrow. Also get going on the exhibits.

Great Neck Library Board meeting tonight.

Lunched with UNESCO group today including George [D.] Stoddard [delegate to UNESCO First General Conference] and Martin Hill. Martin and I got on a first name basis!

March 18, 1950

Cable had gone to University of Cape Town over Palthey's signature. I have telephoned and written to [B.G.]
Fourie [second secretary] of South African [Permanent] Delegation [to U.N.] asking them to second the motion.

I attended yesterday one of the worst meetings or
poorest meetings of my career. It was for setting up a register of candidates for promotion in grades 3-6. Menon of
Personnel was in the chair. All departments, the Secretary-
General's office, and the Library were represented.

The first hour was consumed in beating down the chairman who wanted only as many names as estimated vacancies.
We finally won. I estimated the cost at $400.

Then we took another 1 1/2 hours to discuss the various lists. They had been made up by personnel from lists
submitted by the departments.

The chairman was stubborn, talkative, confusing, out-
wardly pleasant.

Total cost $1000. This, I suppose, is Bureaucracy.

Very soon now I shall have to defend our proposed up-
gradings for the new classification and pay scheme. In preparation for such defense I compiled some figures showing:

	Total Staff	Posts 16 & Above	12 and Above	Administrative Sec- tions or Units, etc.
Library	83	3	9	7
Statistics	90	17	42	5
Finance	98	13	32	7
Personnel	81	10	33	13

All of our 12's and above except 2 12's are chiefs of sections or units, etc.

March 19, 1950

I worked out a memo on the above subject which looks convincing--to me. Hope it does to Cordier and Price.

My contract. The decision Nell and I made 2 or 3 weeks ago still looks like the right one. Reitman knows about it and doesn't like it. da Silva ditto. Hausner by telephone and Heaps in personal conversation appear to accept.

I have written something as a basis for conversation and here follows an outline summary:

A. 1. Health. O. K.
    2. I won on Immelman.
    3. Nell's health. Best to stay 6 months and take Nell south.

B. Successor. I should not choose him but help to find him.
    1. Reitman.
    2. Immelman.
    3. Heaps.
    4. Clapp and Francis
    5. Shall we look inside or outside.
    6. If outside, I'll turn up information if you wish.
    7. If inside--see 1, 2, 3.
    8. Postpone. Hang on to me? Maybe.

C. Possibility of staying on. (Not good)
    1. Leave 1 November. Return 1 April 1951. 1 month here. Do what?
    2. Accept appointment to 1 November 1951. Leave for 6 months. Return 1 May 1951 for 6 months. Budget, building planning, moving, would all be over. It would be the quiet months.
    3. Same as 1, but CHM to return for 2 or 3 weeks every 2d month; or maybe 2 months out of 6. January for settling down in new building; March for budget preparation; April or May for Advisory Committee.

It would give U.N. more time to size up candidates. It would keep me in picture until move is completed and 1952 budget prepared. But it would keep me responsible for the

Library for a year from 1 May 1950, largely in absentia. I
would not be free to do what is best for Nell. At best I
should be free not to come. I might not save anything out of
what I would get because of travel costs.

week.
I hope I can get this settled before the end of this

New York Garden Show begins today.

March 25, 1950

The Woodrow Wilson Library comes to the U.N. The
final vote was 11 to 8. Hail to: Arthur Sweetser, Clyde
Eagleton, Raymond Fosdick, Louise Wright [director, Chicago
Council on Foreign Relations]. But especially and emphatically Arthur Sweetser.

I thought this fight was lost. It was [to be] my one
big defeat. But, thanks largely to A.W.,[38] we finally came
out on top.

Wonder what Julian Boyd [librarian, Princeton University Library] thinks this morning.[39]

My successor. Following talks with Bob Hausner,
Naomi Osborne and Willard Heaps, I find myself thinking that
the best solution might be to get Osborn from Harvard for
1 year, while Reitman, Immelman and Heaps show their stuff.
Can we get Osborn for 1 year? Maybe. I've been lucky so
far.

Have I been lucky!

March 28, 1950

It is about time for me to quit or at least take some
time off. I'm dreaming and thinking U.N. problems at night,
and that's not good. Last night it was Woodrow Wilson Library. Maybe all I need is physical exercise.

About 7 months to go. I must begin seriously to make
notes for Cordier, Price, and/or my successor. (See
Ideas.)[40]

April 4, 1950

Things happen fast. Miss Haskins learned from Osborn he would be willing to come before June--maybe 1 May--
on temporary appointment; would be willing to come as grade
16 more or less permanently with assurance that he would be
my successor! This _is_ good news. Can I put it across? I
would like to. Reitman heard it first from Haskins, fortu-
nately. He told me that if Osborn comes on this basis, he,
Reitman, would not be a candidate.

It seems to be getting around that I'm leaving 1 November. Contract not yet signed but Hausner says there are no
hitches. Apparently I'll be accepted for 6 if I am not available
for 12 months.

I sent the following memo to Price, copy to Cordier,
yesterday, having previously told Bob Hausner, etc. same
things. [41]

Today was spent largely with da Silva and Claire Howe
on problem of reclassification of posts. The former admitted
that, on basis of qualification, all our professionals would be
intermediates, no juniors. But our reclassification is going
to cost too much; we must compromise. We yielded on several points but came out pretty well.

April 8, 1950

Opening of the trout season. Willard Heaps' cocktail
party for his mother.

Passing both up. Nell slept very little last night. I
persuaded her to have bread and milk at noon and go to bed

to eat. She did, and appears to be sound asleep.

Last Wednesday Mr. [H.C.] Kingstone [legal officer, General Legal Division] and I spent a long morning with Redmond [probably Roland L., an attorney with Carter, Ledyard and Milburn] re-drafting contract between Woodrow Wilson Foundation and U.N. No serious disagreement. Draft we made came yesterday p.m. and is now in Reitman's hands.

April 21, 1950

The Bureau of Personnel has got me red hot again. Is my boiling point getting too low or is Palthey a knave and a fool? I might write a memo to Mr. Price somewhat as follows:

> To: Mr. ~~Price~~ [W.P.] Barrett [deputy director, Bureau of Personnel]
>
> From: CHM
>
> Subject: Personnel Problems

I have had another clash with the Bureau of Personnel, another one in a long series of incidents.

In January, 1949, I brought Guido Gomez de Silva into my office as a personal assistant. He had been a grade 8 cataloguer and became a grade 9 in April, 1949. In the 1950 budget the post became administrative officer, grade 11.

I have requested that Gomez be upgraded to an 11. The Bureau of Personnel consents only to a grade 10.

The facts briefly are:

Gomez has 3 degrees, including a library science degree from Columbia University. He speaks English, Spanish, and French fluently, and can manage Portuguese and Italian. He was recommended for his present position by practically all of my principal associates who had known him for a year and one-half.

He did an outstanding job last year as a personal assistant on the professional level.   This year he is also carrying satisfactorily the responsibilities of Executive Officer.
The budget officers find him extraordinarily competent.

If he were 30 instead of 25 I could conscientiously
recommend him for a grade 12 or 13 post as chief of a unit.
Mr. Reitman, after working closely with him for a month,
remarked: "That boy will be the director of the Library
some day. "

He has been offered a post as interpreter, grade 14
I think.   The offer is being renewed, and pressed, from time
to time.

And the Personnel Bureau graciously consents to let
me make him a 10!

The argument appears to be:

Gomez has limited experience as an Executive Officer;
many other administrative officers and assistants have longer
experience and are not yet at grade 11.   His 7 years of successful library experience in Mexico and the U.S. , and the
essentiality of that experience to the performance of his
double duties, appear to be ignored.

It is the general policy to grant only 1 step increase
at a time.

The decision is particularly irksome because it is just
the latest of a long series of Personnel Bureau actions which
prevent operation of the Library at top efficiency.

Most serious was the delay in inviting Immelman to
the grade 16 post as Chief of Processing.   He now declines,
though he would almost certainly have accepted if the offer
had been made last October when he was in this country.
That post--one of our 2 grade 16's--has been vacant since
early June, 1949, except as I have been able to fill it

temporarily from time to time.

Other actions include delays in approving our recommendations for other positions, sometimes for many months, although in the end our first proposal was approved (this happened at least twice) forcing us to take clerks that we knew were incompetent to perform our particular tasks and who were actually fired or transferred a few months later.

Another annoying thing about the Gomez decision is that--unless I misunderstand the regulations--it was taken improperly. Regulation, Chapter 4, Section 3, of the Administrative Manual book calls for action by a promotions board consisting of representatives of Administrative and Financial Services, the Department concerned, and a third department.

This decision was taken at a meeting last week which was attended by Menon, Moltu, Milam, Miss Howe, and Miss Lafferty.

No representative from a third department was present.

Finally, Mr. Menon quite obviously had made his firm decision (or it had been made for him) in advance of the meeting and discussion.

Because of the irregularity of the action, and more particularly because I am profoundly convinced the decision was wrong and, if it stands, will be harmful to the Library and to the U.N., I respectfully appeal for a reversal.

This is a case for recognizing unusual merit and performance.

June 28, 1950

Incidentally my last pay day.

Last Sunday and yesterday were the big days in the Security Council on Korea. The action on both days made me proud of the U.N. and the U.S.

I've finished the notes for my successor and nearly finished my 30 June over-all letter to the Library Advisory Committee.

Bob Lester and Dorothy Loemker [wife of Elmer Loemker, New York book designer] are throwing a party for me at the Coffee House tomorrow night. The staff is having a meeting and a party Friday afternoon.

I've sent a memorandum about the selection of my successor to Price and Cordier, Palthey, Barrett, da Silva, McDiarmid, Luther Evans, M. Cain and a few others.

Library Advisory Committee Friday morning.

Budget hearing comes Thursday p. m. with the Advisory Committee. I'm all but ready and expect no serious difficulties.

Today Reitman and I are lunching with [Olyntho Pinto] Machado [delegate from Brazil and member, Advisory Committee on Administrative and Budgetary Questions] and Bill Hall [U.S. member, Advisory Committee on Administrative and Budgetary Questions].

I've begun seeing people and saying my farewells. So far: Ralph Bunche [principal director, Division of Trusteeship], Jan G. Lindstrom, Maurice Liu [acting chief, Film Section, Department of Public Information], Palthey and Barrett, Mr. [Richard V.] Elms [senior purchase officer, Purchase Section], and Mr. [David] Vaughan [director, Department of Conference and General Services].

NOTES

[1]This is the first entry in the diary, indicating that the following six entries were recorded after the date of the events they relate. Milam used a great many abbreviations and truncations in his diary. These have been spelled out to assist the reader. Punctuation has also been added where necessary to clarify meaning. Misspellings have been corrected. Ellipses have been used to indicate repetitive material that has been deleted by the editor. All names of persons are identified in brackets the first time the name appears in the diary. If no identification is made, the editor has been unable to identify the person. Positions given are in the United Nations unless otherwise designated.

[2]The library then reported to the Bureau of Technical Services, which was in the Department of Conference and General Services.

[3]Ralph A. Beals, Luther H. Evans, Carl H. Milam, and A. C. Breycha-Vauthier, "Report: Planning of United Nations Library," 22-23 April 1947. See Appendix A.

[4]Verner W. Clapp, "Quantities of Materials Required by United Nations Library," 3 May 1947. John E. Burchard, "Proposal A: Estimate of Space Requirements for U.N. Library, New York City," 5 May 1947; and "Proposal B: Estimate of Space Requirements for UN Library, New York City," 5 May 1947.

[5]Ralph R. Shaw, Library and Documentation Services of the United Nations (Lake Success: 12 September 1947). The Introduction and Chapter IV and V of this report are included in Appendix B.

[6]Letter from Benjamin Cohen, January 22, 1948, asking Milam to serve as a full-time consultant to the United Nations Library until the end of the year.

[7]This refers to the continuation of notes of February 5 rather than to those of February 6.

[8]The Universal Decimal Classification was used for official publications, and the Library of Congress classification system was used for nonofficial publications.

[9]Dr. Sevensma, who had been librarian of the League of Nations from 1927 to 1938 and librarian of the University of Leyden from 1938 to 1947, prematurely announced at an Association of Research Libraries meeting in New York on November 28, 1947, that he had accepted the post of director of the United Nations Libraries. For a fuller account of this incident see Doris Cruger Dale, The United Nations Library: Its Origins and Development (Chicago: American Library Association, 1970), pp. 38-39.

[10]This is the date on which Milam started the diary. Evidently the extensive notes of February 5 and 6 were recorded on this date.

[11]Letter from Mary G. Smieton, director of personnel, United Nations, offering Milam "the post of Director of Libraries in our Department of Public Information," dated February 19, 1948.

[12]Telegram from Benjamin Cohen, March 3, 1948, suggesting that Milam come to New York to consult on budgetary and other urgent matters concerning the library.

[13]On March 5, Milam wrote to Luther Evans and Verner Clapp, soliciting their advice about the organization of the library, about budgetary matters, and about special equipment. This entry refers to their reply.

[14]The name Erikson is written in the margin. This could be Reinholdt A. L. Eriksen, deputy executive officer, Department of Public Information.

[15]List of questions was not included in the diary.

[16]Milam alternately spelled his surname Wyck and Wijk.

[17]This letter was not in the diary. It was located in the Milam papers and is reprinted in Appendix C.

[18]The remainder of the notes for April 10 consist of

a detailed description of a house-hunting trip on Long Island.

[19]Both the morning and the afternoon of April 11 were devoted to house hunting.

[20]The remaining notes for May 16 consist of an item-ized account of Milam's consultant fees, travel expenses, and salary checks.

[21]Notes in the margin of diary: "Note of 29 October. Nell bought a lovely raincoat 40.00. I bought reel and line 18.87. 58.87. So the account is closed. Abercrombie and Fitch tells me rod costs $60.00!"

[22]His speech was later published in the ALA Bulletin. See Appendix D.

[23]Both of these men were associated with Milam in the A.L.A. Library War Service.

[24]Notes for this date were devoted to a recapitulation of income and travel expenses.

[25]This is the only typewritten entry in the diary. It is again devoted to a summary of income and travel expenses.

[26]The Division of Library Services as of 1 January 1949. (Lake Success: 1 January 1949). This was the first annual report issued by the library. See Appendix E.

[27]Helen E. Wessells. "Report: Notes for a Check List of Projects Under Way or Projected by the United Nations: To Be Evaluated to Determine the Implications for Library Services," (ca. 1948).

[28]The reference is to a conference regarding library internships.

[29]The appointments of both Osborn and Heaps were on a temporary basis only.

[30]This fund consisted of gifts to the League of Nations Library.

[31]These pages read as follows: "A Book on U.N. See diary 10 July 1949. Part I. What the U.N. does. a. His-torical note, with some reference to League. b. The U.N.

as a political organization. Power vs. mediation. Achieve-
ments. c. The U.N. in Economic Field. d. The U.N. in
Social Field   Part II. How to organize an experimental U.N.
a. General Assembly. b. Security Council. c. Economic and
Social Council. d. Trusteeship Council.   Part III. Bibliography. Procedure. 1. First I should assemble all books and
pamphlets written about the U.N. Maybe I'll find that what I
propose has already been done. 2. If not, then I should start
my: a. Selected bibliography. b. Selected collection of material." Milam never wrote this book, but after he left the
United Nations he wrote a long article about the library which
was published in Library Quarterly. See Appendix F.

[32]A personnel regulation providing for temporary appointments.

[33]This note, although out of chronological order, was
inserted here by Milam in order to answer the questions he
had posed on December 6.

[34]No further notes were added at this point.

[35]This name is crossed out in the diary.

[36]Inserted here is a diet given to Milam by his doctor.

[37]This appears to be an error and probably should
read February 17.

[38]This seems to be a mistake. It is obvious that
Milam is referring to Arthur Sweetser, who at this time was
director of the United Nations Information Center in Washington. Formerly he had been chairman of the Woodrow Wilson
Foundation (1943 to 1945). From 1918 to 1932 he was a member of the Information Section of the League of Nations, one
of the few Americans who remained with the League after the
United States failed to join.

[39]See entry for July 1, 1949. It seems that Princeton
had previously objected to the transfer of the Woodrow Wilson
Library.

[40]Five pages of notes at the end of the diary. Notes
are dated February or March, 1948; April 20-21, 1949?;
March 28, 1950. Some are undated. They refer to matters
already discussed in the diary, so are not inserted here.

[41]This memo is not included in the diary.

REPORT: PLANNING OF UNITED NATIONS LIBRARY
Meeting of Library Consultants
April 22 and 23, 1947.

Mr. Ralph A. Beals, Director, New York Public Library
Mr. Luther H. Evans, Librarian of Congress
Mr. Carl H. Milam, Executive Secretary, American
    Library Association
Mr. A. C. Breycha-Vauthier, Librarian, United Nations
    Library, Geneva

I.   The Library Consultants believe that the United Nations
must have a library service of the most advanced type, spe-
cially developed to meet the particular needs of the Secretariat, organs of the United Nations, the Delegations and the
Specialized Agencies.

II. They believe that the emphasis should be on reference,
bibliographical and documentation services, including detailed
analysis of many important publications, rather than on accumulation and preservation of great stocks of books.

III. This concept of library service envisages a staff adequate
in number and competent in subject specialization to make surveys of the literature of problems in all fields, analyse its
basic factual material, assemble statements of alternative
opinions and arguments by contestants and subject authorities;
in other words to do a considerable amount of the preliminary
assembling, weeding and analyzing of the required material.

IV. As to materials, the library must include:

1. Complete files of the documents of all kinds pub-
    lished and unpublished, of United Nations, and of all
    the specialized agencies and commissions, including
    the official archives of U.N. if so required.

2. Extensive yet highly selected collections, with

emphasis on recent material of documents, periodicals, pamphlets, newspapers and clippings, books,
processed reports and studies, maps, pictures,
sound records, films, etc. on:

a. Each member state.
b. Other nations.
c. All subjects with which United Nations deals,
    such as: Treaties, Government, Law, military
    affairs, atomic energy, economics, finance,
    transportation, communication, agriculture, sta-
    tistics, health, human rights, social welfare,
    displaced persons, etc., etc.

In this category, the criterion for acquisition
and retention should be usefulness to the United
Nations. When materials are no longer used
frequently, they should be removed from the
active files.

V. Much of the library service must be provided to United
Nations personnel in their own offices. Temporary and even
permanent small deposits of frequently used material will be
needed in several departments and in the delegation building.
The same would have to apply on a larger scale in case Specialized Agencies decide to establish their headquarter or
branch offices on the Secretariat Site. The most economical
and efficient means of providing such service will be through
a completely centralized administration of all United Nations'
library resources and library services.

VI. The United Nations Library should cooperate with other
libraries to the end that all library resources should be made
quickly available to the United Nations when needed. Such
guides to the resources of these libraries as are now available
should be supplemented with the special needs of United Nations
in mind.

VII. Bibliographical services provided currently to the Secretariat, the Delegations and the Specialized Agencies should
include:

1. Lists of accessions.

2. Frequent lists on subjects of current importance to
    United Nations including all types of materials.

3. Current abstracting service on special topics as
    required.

All of these services should be made available in suitable form to libraries and scholars throughout the world.

VIII. The principal library collections and services should be easily accessible to all of the United Nations civil services, delegations and particularly to the Secretariat. Because of the impossibility of determining now or soon the exact amount of space which will ultimately be required, the building should be an independent or semi-independent structure. This appears to indicate a wing attached to the building for the Secretariat. This wing should be so planned that expansion of both stack and reading room space will be possible. Modern facilities for easy intercommunication and transportation of materials in the Secretariat and between buildings on the Site should be incorporated in the plan.

IX. The library should be planned for maximum freedom of access by authorized readers, to books, pamphlets, periodicals and other materials.

X. The consultants recommend that a competent librarian be engaged to make a quick estimate of the quantities of materials which will probably be needed in each important subject field and geographical area to serve the needs of the United Nations and Specialized Agencies so as to draw up a preliminary budget of the approximate number of volumes which would meet the requirements set forth in this report.

XI. The consultants recommend that a competent library expert be engaged immediately to translate the requirements of the library into a building program and a list of space requirements.

XII. They agree with the frequently expressed opinion of members of the Secretariat that the library building should be ready for use when the Secretariat building is occupied.

Appendix B

[Excerpts from]
LIBRARY AND DOCUMENTATION SERVICES
OF THE UNITED NATIONS

[Ralph R. Shaw]

12 September 1947

Introduction

The problems with which the United Nations deals are global in scope and it is not possible to make on-the-spot investigations the basis for all decisions. The intelligence contained in the world's literature, therefore, constitutes a fundamental basis for sound operation of the substantive programs of the United Nations, and the library and bibliographical service needs of the United Nations are of greatest urgency.

Evidence abounds that the work of the substantive staff of the United Nations has been seriously hampered by lack of adequate library service, and the library does not contend that it is able to do the job now or that it will be able adequately to provide the services needed for current work within the next four to six years.

Despite liberal provision for library service during the last year, as compared with the funds generally available for such services in research libraries and scholarly institutions, and despite fantastically liberal provision for the library and bibliographical services in the budget for 1948, it is contended that it will not be possible to provide the services required in 1948 or for several years thereafter! The excuses offered are newness of the organization, frequent changes in space, lack of personnel, confusion in policy, need for time to build up a large bookstock, difficulties in recruiting personnel, etc. These have unquestionably been serious problems. Nevertheless, even after liberal allowance is made for these factors, it appears that the present library operation is a model of inefficiency, waste, and blundering; that time and more money will not cure all its ills; and that fundamental recasting of the

operation and its reorientation to sound management and a
philosophy of dynamic service are essential. If this is done
it should speedily be possible to develop a service agency
which will meet a large part of the literature needs of the
staff of the United Nations at a fraction of the expenditure
proposed for 1948.

The minimum requirements for library and bibliographical services which must and can be met in the near future
are:

1. Speedy access to publications consulted frequently.
Publications used more or less constantly by any staff member should be on his desk as part of his working equipment
and publications used as frequently as quarterly by the Secretariat should be in the United Nations Library and should be
available to any staff member within ten or fifteen minutes.

2. Reference services which promptly provide any
factual information which can be determined from literature.

3. Current literature service to keep the staff aware
of world events and problems of interest to the United Nations.
This includes arrangements for routing of periodicals and
newspapers to staff members to call to their attention auto-
matically the world thought and information which must be
part of their intellectual equipment if they are to be effective
members of the Secretariat. As a second step it would be
highly desirable to issue a current annotated bibliography covering the literature of interest to the Secretariat, the specialized agencies and other international groups, and, possibly,
to provide an adequate clipping service.

4. Intensive indexing of the publications of the United
Nations and, as soon as possible, of the publications of other
international bodies so that the library will constitute a basic
research resource in the work of international organizations.

5. Stocks of United Nations and other international organizations' publications adequate to provide for all reference
and circulation needs of the Secretariat.

6. Research services, including arrangements by which
the total literature of the world can be made available to the
Secretariat Commissions, Delegations, and others, when they
are dealing with crucial world problems. This should include
full utilization of the great literature research potential of the

New York-Washington area and the development of working arrangements to this end with the great research libraries of the vicinity, as well as generous use of auxiliary methods such as photoduplication, and similar scholarly library services.

7. The provision of recreational and training literature for the staff to stimulate them to continuing intellectual development and enlarged usefulness in the United Nations program. As noted in the report which follows, these objectives can be achieved in large measure in the immediate future, at a fraction of the expenditures budgeted for 1948. They will not be achieved in five or even ten years, even if several times the 1948 budget is provided, if the library and bibliographical development of the United Nations continues on its present course and at its current rate of productivity.

[Here follows Chapter I, "Government and Policies," 44 double-spaced typed pages; Chapter II, "Management of the Library," 42pp.; and Chapter III, "Departmental Libraries," 8pp.]

Chapter IV

RELATIONS WITH OTHER LIBRARIES

Almost unanimously the libraries in New York as well as the Library of Congress, in Washington, have offered to do everything they possibly can to help the United Nations carry out its program. This has been a fine demonstration of whole hearted interest in the purpose for which the United Nations was created.

Among the unusual privileges granted by libraries to the United Nations were long-term loans of considerable collections from the Library of Congress, New York University Library and the Carnegie Endowment for International Peace.

A large part of the collections loaned to the United Nations are still on hand in its Circulation Section. In addition, the Reference Department of the New York Public Library, a private organization with regulations forbidding the loan of publications outside its building, has loaned more books to the United Nations during the last few months than it had loaned to all others in its history.

Surprisingly enough, these manifestations of interest
and good will and the desire of these and other libraries to
help the United Nations at their own expense have been met
with half-hearted acceptance and with suspicion on the part of
responsible officials of the United Nations. Such statements
as that in the minutes of the 10th Advisory Committee meeting
that it was "felt that it would not be advisable to make arrangements with only one library as there would be no com-
petition..." and the often repeated or implied suggestion that
these libraries expect to get something from the United Nations, show a complete lack of understanding of the philosophy
of American librarianship and the service policies of these libraries.

This suspicious attitude is not confined to the libraries
with whom the United Nations has relations but is also shown
in the discussion of the reports of Mr. Clapp and Mr. Burchard, two experts from whom the Department requested advice. When this advice was contrary to the building program
previously decided upon, serious questions were raised as to
the motives of these men.

All told, the relationship of the United Nations to other
libraries has been clearly limited by the United Nations' own
failure to realize that services offered were just normal library services courteously extended to the United Nations because of the great interest in the United Nations' program.

Failure to utilize these services has materially handi-
capped the work of the substantive staff of the United Nations.

Libraries had offered these services freely and without
charge, and have encountered speculation as to what they
wanted from the United Nations. It is recommended that not
only should these offers of service be gratefully accepted as
exceedingly valuable aids, but, what is more, the United Nations should offer to pay the full cost of such services. It
will receive several times the value that it could obtain from
an equal amount invested in its own library.

It should be noted that in almost no case have the offers of cooperation from the various libraries been accepted
fully and effectively by the United Nations.

One of the aspects of the use of other libraries that
has been stressed repeatedly by the librarian is the limited
length of loans allowed by these libraries. Upon checking

with 5 of the 6 libraries most frequently used by the United Nations it was found that there had been no serious attempt to arrive at an understanding for the categories of loans needed for longer periods.

Miss Savord, the librarian of the Council of Foreign Relations, reported that there had been no serious discussion of longer term loans, and that the Council will be perfectly willing to loan any book which is not in constant use for 6 months or longer subject to recall if the Council needs it.

The College of the City of New York was approached by Mr. Gerould more than a year ago on the question of loans, but has never been asked for the loan of any book. Its librarian, Mr. Wilcox, says that he would be glad to take up with his President the question of long-term loans for Secretariat staff under the same conditions as such loans are made to the University faculty, if the United Nations indicates the need for such services. The New York Public Library and others indicated also that loans could be made for more than one week if desired.

The New York Public Library has even gone so far as to offer to put one of their reference staff members at the disposal of the United Nations, without charge, to delve into reference questions. Despite the fact that the Library Advisory Committee repeatedly recommended the assignment of one of the United Nations own staff to answer questions from the collections of the New York Public Library, this and other offers from the New York Public Library has not apparently merited a reply.

The librarians of other libraries also indicated that their relations with the United Nations were not particularly good. Columbia points out that the U.N. Library frequently does not verify its references when it requests the loan of publications. Normal inter-library loan courtesy requires that the Library requesting a loan undertake the verification of a reference if this is at all possible. There is evidence that the Reference Section attempts to do that if it can be done from the limited reference tools at hand.

Another example of bungling of relations between the United Nations Library and the New York Public Library was in the provision of special work space in the New York Public Library for the United Nations. Mr. Pelt arranged with Mr. Beals, the Director of the New York Public Library for space

in which staff of the United Nations could work, using type-
writers and secretarial assistance. Shortly thereafter a misunderstanding arose. Instead of checking up on the matter,
Mr. Rasmussen sent out a memorandum reporting there had
apparently been a misunderstanding and that no such space was
to be provided in the New York Public Library. Upon investigation it was found that there actually is a large room next
to the Economics Department which was and still is available
to the staff of the United Nations and it has not been used because the staff was informed that no such space was provided.

Summary

The only way in which the United Nations can effectively strengthen its substantive programs and supply the
literature needed for its work immediately and in the future
is to make the fullest possible use of the existent facilities.
Serious investigation shows that the libraries of New York
are apparently far more willing to serve the United Nations
than the United Nations has been willing to accept the services
provided.

It is recommended that the United Nations make maximum possible use of other libraries, particularly the New
York Public Library, and that it undertake to pay the costs
of such services so that it will not cause an undue drain upon
the service facilities of the cooperating libraries. The library
best suited to provide the intensive dynamic services the
United Nations needs is the Reference Department of the New
York Public Library.

Chapter V

PROGRAM FOR THE FUTURE

The recommendations which follow are based upon the following premises:

1. The United Nations must have library service ade-
    quate fully to meet its day-to-day needs.
2. The United Nations should assume responsibility for
    collection and organization of the world's primary
    research collection of publications of international
    organizations.
3. That the fundamental philosophy underlying the oper-
    ation of the library must be that it is to be a

service agency rather than an end in itself; that it
will therefore, stress documentation services and
use of available resources, rather than the building
up of a collection of large proportions primarily for
the sake of building up a large library.

As has been pointed out in this report, the United Nations is spending excessive amounts for library and bibliographical services and, what is worse, is not getting services
adequate to support its substantive programs. One-third of
the more than $900,000 budgeted for these purposes for 1948
should be sufficient, if properly used, to provide superior
service in the immediate future.

To make maximum use of its library and bibliographical funds, U.N. should make as full use as possible of existent resources and services. For example, it appears inex-
cusable to withhold books from use and to do an expensive job
of cataloguing them, when the great bulk of them have already
been added to libraries such as the New York Public Library
and Columbia University Library, and sets of cards could be
copied from the files of these libraries for a very small fraction of the cost of original cataloguing done in the U.N. Library. Acquisition of general publications too, could be done
for a small fraction of the present cost by contract with a library that buys efficiently and has already looked up the necessary information in buying its own copy. Contractual services with the Reference Department of the New York Public
Library could immediately make the great resources of that
institution available on the U.N. site to the entire Secretariat.

Certain categories of service should not be obtained by
contract. These include intensive documentation services
based on the U.N.'s own publications and those of other international organizations; compilation of special bibliographies
and lists needed by the Secretariat or agencies of the U.N.,
and the collecting and organization of the U.N.'s primary research collection in the field of publications of international
organizations.

The library program of the U.N. is discussed in two
phases: A--what should be done immediately and B--what
should be done at the permanent headquarters. A--The immediate needs of the U.N. for dynamic library services can
best be met by:

1.   Transfer and combination of all library and bibliographical

services to a single library in the Department of Public Information.

2. Reduction of the budget to $300,000 for 1948, with approximately $100,000 available for contractual services with the New York Public Library and $200,000 available for building up the collection of international documentation and providing specialized indexing and bibliographic services in the field of publications of international organizations.

3. Engage the most competent librarian available in the world, paying $10,000 per year, as proposed in the budget, to ensure maximum utilization of all available resources for immediate as well as long range objectives.

4. Transfer from Geneva to headquarters of the publications of the various international organizations to form the nucleus of U.N.'s research collection in that field. Since there are many collections of such publications in the great research libraries of Europe, that will not reduce European research potential.

5. Transfer of the remainder of the Geneva Library to UNESCO or to organizations which can make them of maximum usefulness to European cultural rehabilitation, and retention of only such materials at Geneva as are proven requisite to the needs of U.N. at that point.

6. Contract with the Reference Department of the New York Public Library for general reference services, the maintenance of a good, live, reference collection at U.N. headquarters and the use of its 3,000,000 volumes in a special reading room at Lake Success.

B--Library Service for the permanent site.

1. Arrange for a branch of the New York Public Library in a suitable location in the U.N. building. This should make available a large potential of recreational, reference, and training material to the staff at the U.N. as well as to the general public at no cost to the U.N. except for the maintenance of approximately 20,000 square feet of space.

2. Continue the arrangements recommended above as step A.

These recommendations if followed will immediately increase the library service to the Secretariat of the U.N., will save $600,000 per year, and will put the U.N. in position of rendering world service in the documentation of international organizations.

[The report ends here.]

18 March 1948

TO MEMBERS OF [U.N.] LIBRARY STAFF

I regret that I was unable last week to meet and talk with all of you.

During the four days I was at Lake Success it seemed desirable to concentrate on (1) Library Policy, (2) Budget, and on (3) Relations with persons in the Secretariat who can help the Library Services to become what they ought to be.

1.   The preliminary policy statement was evolved primarily in meetings with Messrs. Timperley, Naprstek, Rasmussen and Reitman. Briefly it states:

That emphasis is to be on service, not on accumulation of a large stock of books;
That the service is primarily for the official family, but that the needs of the press and of scholars interested in UN must be recognized;
That, as to materials, we should obtain and process first what is most relevant and urgent, and most likely to be used.

2.   The Budgets of the various units were considered in detail. It was agreed that a high priority should be given to a stenographic-typist pool;
That the detailed budget will be presented by Mr. Timperley in the light of our discussions and after further conference with his associates.

3.   Good Relations with the Secretariat outside the Library are obviously essential. I therefore spent a large part of my limited time in seeing officials of the DPI, and persons in other departments and bureaus who are concerned with budget, management and personnel.

They explained limitations and difficulties with an obvious desire to help the Library, and also with hope and some assurance that the problems will be solved and the difficulties largely overcome. I could not have asked for a finer appreciation of the potentialities of the Library Services.

We also had a profitable meeting with the Library Committee. I am sure the members of this group also will cooperate fully in our efforts to provide the best possible service.

I asked the members of that Committee to send their criticisms and suggestions for our consideration after May 1. I now extend the same invitation to each of you.

Purely Personal--I have been in touch with the UN housing people, and have made my housing needs known to several friends. But I am sure I can use more scouts.

We are two, or at times, three adults. We need two bedrooms. Small cottage much preferred, but may have to take an apartment. Unfurnished preferred. Within driving distance of Lake Success. No objection to country or small village. Rent $100.00 to $150.00, if possible. Occupancy on or about May 1. Lease one year or two.

I am not asking you to take on this extra burden, but if something happens to turn up I hope you will let Mrs. Compton know.

I'll be seeing you soon.

Cordially yours

Carl H. Milam

Appendix D

MILAM, THE INTERNATIONALIST

Harry M. Lydenberg*

Carl Milam, Internationalist brings to mind a chat we two had at one of the A. L. A. conventions as we strolled-- no, strode is the better word for a man trying to keep up with Carl Milam--from one meeting to another, talking about him and his future, whether he did well by the Association in staying on as Secretary or whether it would be better to let someone else take his place there and he accept one of the posts calling for constructive reorganization and development, one of the calls that came to him at no infrequent intervals. Pros and cons he urged on both sides, all held up with char- acteristic dispassionateness and objectiveness.

"I've got imagination enough to take it on," he said, "if I've got nothing else. That's one thing I think I could use helpfully there, knowing and understanding how the other fel- low feels, trying to be guided by some such beacon."

Yes, I was quite willing to admit his possession of imagination, ability to look forward, willingness to listen and then go ahead on his own. And it seems to me that in few of his many other activities has he shown his strength better than in the field of the relations of the library world of this country with the work in other lands.

At first sight one might think this international side of our work would be of lesser or little interest to him. Here's a man born in Kansas, his whole adolescent and early adult life spent in the South and Midwest. See how slight were the incidental--and therefore important--suggestions about activi- ties in other lands. I don't know just when he saw salt water

*Reprinted by permission of the American Library Association from the ALA Bulletin 42, 9 (15 September 1948), 5-6. This paper was read at the third ALA general session, June 17, 1948, by Milton E. Lord (director, Boston Public Library).

first or crossed the border, but I'm sure it came well after
he cast his first vote. Probably his first intimate and extensive experience with overseas work came when, with Mal-
colm Wyer, he served as an assistant to Dr. Putnam in connection with our Army libraries in 1917-18. Then he saw
plenty of books go overseas, plenty of librarians follow them
for service, but he stayed home, busy with the foundation work
for "books in the war."

That war to end war came to its end. That Army work
of the Association came to its end. Then came the call to be
Secretary of the national association and came the move to
Chicago, came the development of work with the new hand on
the wheel. Perhaps the pressure was not quite so strong in
those days, the contacts with foreign libraries not quite so
extensive and exacting, the sense of our responsibility for
meeting the demand from other lands for information and advice about so many phases of library work, all this is a little
less insistent perhaps then than it became later. I'm sure
the calls came, however, heavy enough at the time, growing
day by day, and it is not a bit troublesome to picture the
scene if they had been met by a less sympathetic and less
understanding personality.

From those distant days, more than a quarter-century
ago, down to the very present, the work with foreign friends
has grown, at times demanding more attention than our do-
mestic problems. And goodness knows that the latter were
ever present, even more than snappingly insistent for settle-
ment. Nor can we forget how widespread and vocal was the
mood that reminded us that we had problems of our own, that
we had plenty of need for service of books to hundreds of
thousands of our own people quite without library service.
"America first" was not only a slogan, but an ever present
and movingly vocal cry, certainly deserving attention if not
being put in first rank. All in all, the new Secretary found
he needed balance as well as sympathy.

And it was in just that control over impulses and emo-
tions, in just that sense of balance between what he saw on
our own door step and what he glimpsed of affairs abroad,
that Carl Milam showed one of his most important and char-
acteristic abilities. He never failed to remember how many
in our own land had no adequate library service, never failed
to plead the cause of better education for librarianship, never
forgot that unless we encourage library extension we feel the
beginning of senility and decay. I could go on and name other

sides of our work at home more dear to the hearts of each
of us, but there is no need to spread them all before you.
With never a suggestion of trying to carry water on both
shoulders, with perfect willingness to take his stand and hold
his position when the occasion demanded, he, nevertheless,
remembered and understood that we are just as much our
brother's keeper when he calls from abroad as when he stands
up as a member of our immediate family.

At the moment I recall no meeting of the Association
on foreign soil, no international library gathering, no time
when a welcome was needed for visitors from overseas, when
Carl Milam has not been the spirit moving the participation
or developing the best way to give the foreigner what he needs.
After the Atlantic City Conference in 1926 he helped conduct
the foreign visitors through the country. It was at a meeting
of that group in Washington that there was first discussed the
movement that later developed into the International Federation of Library Associations. The A. L. A. was then formally
asked by the group to serve as a committee to bring in a plan
at the Edinburgh meeting in 1927.

The International Library Committee was formed at the
Edinburgh meeting in 1927, later to become the federation.
After Edinburgh, he attended the meetings in Rome and Venice
in 1929, and Spain in 1935. And at the UNESCO conference
at Paris in 1946 his voice was equally potent.

He was honored by the decoration given him by the King
of Sweden after the 1926 conference, by an honorary member-
ship in the Academia Nacional de Ciencias Antonio Alzate of
Mexico, by the Asociación de Bibliotecarios y Bibliógrafos de
España, and served on too many working committees on international affairs during the Second World War to call for men-
tion here.

It was my good fortune to be with him in 1944 on a
trip through Latin America, and my good fortune to see how
admirably he met the conditions that faced us, often widely
different from what we had expected or imagined. Just one
more indication of the man's imagination and his sense of
balance, of his good--nay, excellent!--common sense.

I wish that you here heard him tell some of his im-
pressions of things abroad. Ask him what he thinks of the
fun of trying for a driver's permit in Switzerland with a car
bought in France. Ask him to tell what he thinks of the

charming and picturesque seaport of Valparaiso and the speed
and international understanding of the tailors down there when
faced with the problem of Yankee zippers. Ask him--but I've
run along too much. Get him in a corner and have him tell
some of his experiences in his own way, and I'm sure you
will be quite content to forget these words and to listen to
his own. None of you listeners now, however, can surpass
in sincerity and intensity the feeling of admiration for Carl
Milam the internationalist held by the man who writes these
lines. The United Nations may not know now full well how
fortunate the organization is in the choice of its librarian,
but we all with no exception are more than willing to join in
hearty congratulation for its good fortune in his acceptance
and in heartiest confidence that under his guidance and leader-
ship its library work looks forward to a happy and successful
future.

Appendix E

THE [U.N.] DIVISION OF LIBRARY SERVICES
AS OF 1 JANUARY 1949*

Carl H. Milam

The United Nations Library is making fair progress.
We have added quite a lot of books and documents during recent months, in many languages, from many countries, on
many subjects, and have catalogued as many as we could.
Current periodicals are now available in the reading room.
Many United Nations documents and some periodicals have
been bound. We have added a few very useful staff members.
We are getting good (but limited) bibliographical service from
the Library of Congress and the New York Public Library
under contract. The United Nations Document Checklists and
Indexes for early sessions are nearing completion. A weekly
subject index to United Nations and Specialized Agency Documents publications is--we hope--just around the corner. A
current pamphlet file has been started which may become one
of the most useful parts of the whole Library.

We have had good support from our Department and
from the Secretariat as a whole. The Advisory Committee
on Administrative and Budgetary Questions and the Fifth Committee have responded sympathetically to our proposals. We
still have a long way to go, and we still need your criticisms
and constructive suggestions.

Policy. The Division has a working policy which was
arrived at on the advice of many consultants and is based
largely on the Report of the International Advisory Committee
of Library Experts (A/C.5/222). It is to provide the best
possible reference and documentation service without building
up a great collection of books. Emphasis is on service, not
on accumulation and preservation; on the needs of today and
tomorrow, not on the needs which may possibly arise in the
distant future.

_____
*Addressed "To: The Members of the Permanent Advisory
Library Committee" and dated January 1, 1949

The nearest approach to an official policy will presumably be found in paragraphs 132, 133, and 135 of the Advisory
Committee's Report of 1948 to the General Assembly (A/598),
which were singled out for specific approval by the Fifth Committee. That Committee expects the Secretary-General to
submit a proposed policy for consideration by itself and by
the Assembly in 1949. The preparation of notes for the Secretary-General on this subject is a high priority task of the
Director and his associates during the next few months.

It must be recognized that it will be difficult to adhere
to this policy. If members of the Secretariat and others who
use our services find it necessary to insist on having everything they need at once rather than within 24 or 48 hours; on
having most books and documents for a long time instead of
for a week or two; and if they find it impossibly inconvenient
to work in other libraries even when the books they want are
assembled for them in special study rooms in advance--then
the Library will be forced to request funds and staff for a
large collection. We hope this will not happen.

The Collections may be briefly discussed in three
groups.

First are the books, maps and documents which have
been taken into our permanent collection. They are books for
general reference; books, documents and bound periodicals
dealing with the specific subjects under study by or relevant
to the interests of the United Nations; publications and documents of the League of Nations, the United Nations and the
Specialized Agencies; selected books and pamphlets on international organization. We estimate our holdings in this group
at approximately seventy-five thousand volumes. Substantial
additions have been made in 1948.

Equal in importance are the periodicals, document
serials and newspapers. We currently receive approximately
6,050 titles. About 1,450 of them are obtained on subscrip-
tion; the rest come as gifts or on exchange. Many of these
are routed to the Secretariat on arrival. We are now getting
one additional copy of each of more than 100 titles for exclu-
sive use in the Reading Room.

The third category may be referred to as "unabsorbed
materials." In this group are more than 100,000 items, public documents, periodicals, pamphlets, some books received
as gifts or as parts of large collections, from which final

selections for our permanent stock have not yet been made.
It is anticipated that a great many of these items will eventually be disposed of.   The inability of the staff as at present
constituted to select, catalogue, and bind needed publications
from this large collection and at the same time to take care
of current acquisitions of high priority, constitutes a serious
handicap to the improvement of the service.   Until the cataloguing staff is enlarged this backlog will not only remain but
may continue to grow.

Reclassification.   The use of two separate classifica-
tions, one for books and another for government documents,
was discontinued in the middle of 1948.   Now we use only the
Universal Decimal, following the Geneva library practice.
But we have not been able to reclassify the materials previously classified under the Library of Congress system.

Acquisition Policy.   We apply our general policy to acquisitions by challenging every proposal with the question:
Will the publication be used soon and often?   If the answer is
in the negative, we do not buy except under unusual circum-
stances.   We are similarly challenging the usefulness of materials received as gifts and on exchange; and if the answer
is negative we do not catalogue or bind.

In spite of this policy, it will be obvious to anyone
who thinks about the matter that the needs of the Secretariat,
Delegations and Commissions cannot be met except by a fairly
substantial collection.   We need a few basic reference books
from every country--dictionaries, encyclopedias, statistical
yearbooks, biographical dictionaries, directories, atlases,
gazeteers, brief histories, laws, treaties, etc.... It was
easy to get such books from a few countries.   We are now
engaged in an effort to get such publications from and about
all the others.

Another main category is the current and recent material needed for the day-by-day work of the Secretariat and
other groups.   We estimate that in 1948 publications have
been urgently required on at least 250 major subjects.   The
subjects range from Palestine and the Italian Colonies to
Berlin and Korea; from atomic energy to child welfare and
freedom of the press.   For historical research and for most
of the old publications needed, we must depend on other libraries.   But we cannot borrow the current books, documents
and periodicals on these subjects because, when they are
needed by our people, they are also in great demand by

readers in other libraries. This category will continue indefinitely to require annual allocations, the amount depending
largely on the number and character of the problems which
are considered by the United Nations and of the projects assigned to the Secretariat and other groups for investigation.

Service to Readers. The number of readers in the
Library is not a satisfactory measure of library use. Although a very considerable amount of research work is carried on by members of the Secretariat and others in the
reading room, a vastly larger amount is conducted in the offices of members of the Secretariat with materials from the
Library. It is the business of the acquisition, reference and
circulation librarians and of the departmental liaison librarians
to find the needed documents, books and periodicals and to
make them available. It is my impression that members of
the Library staff have some part in practically every research
project carried on within the organization.

Although the number of inquiries and problems brought
up during the summer and while the Assembly was in session
showed a decrease, the reduction was somewhat less than had
been anticipated. The requests for assistance in fairly extensive bibliographical projects have been surprisingly numerous
and are largely beyond our capacity.

A very large percentage of reference questions can be
answered only from the documents of the United Nations, the
Specialized Agencies, the League of Nations and sovereign
states. It is particularly essential to have the documents in
the first three categories not only complete, but also in very
accessible form, in duplicate or triplicate, and adequately in-
dexed. This goal is far from having been realized. One important step has been taken this year, namely to have sets of
United Nations documents bound. We are continually working
to complete our files; and progress is being made in the
preparation and publication of indexes. Insofar as the resources available to us have permitted, we have made considerable progress in the acquisition of the documents of
sovereign states in those subject fields which are of interest
to the Secretariat. The problem of making these publications
more readily accessible to our readers is one to which we
are giving much thought.

Departmental Collections. Officers of the Division endorse the decision previously made to keep these collections
small, to have them and departmental liaison librarians under

the administration of this Division, to insist on complete co-ordination with the main Library. But we are also aware of the need for better service in Departmental Libraries than we are now able to give. One such library has a librarian and two assistants; and they give good service. Each of the other four is operated by one person; and the service is less good than it should be, no matter how hard that one person works. We therefore endorse the recommendation of the International Advisory Committee of Library Experts that each should be manned by a minimum of two persons, one librarian and one clerk. There is no prospect that our position on this matter should be greatly modified by the move to New York in 1950 or 1951. However, it is possible that one or two additional departmental collections will be necessary when we occupy the new quarters.

Assembly Reference Library. The Division has operated a special reference library for the Assembly in Paris in 1948 as was done previously by the DPI reference center at Flushing. Its books and documents were drawn from headquarters, Geneva and the libraries of Paris; and some books were purchased in Paris to meet needs as they developed. The staff consisted of Mrs. Ravage, from the headquarters Service to Readers Unit, Miss Scanlon, of the Carnegie Endowment Library in Washington, Miss Molesworth, from the Royal Institute of International Affairs in London, and three other assistants. It is assumed that similar service will be needed at future meetings of the Assembly wherever they are held.

Some members of the staffs of the Opinion Survey Section and the Documents Index Unit were also on duty in Paris during the General Assembly meeting.

Library Quarters at Lake Success are reasonably adequate except in two respects. We ought to have at least 50% more reading space at the earliest possible moment, for the convenience of readers. We should also be provided soon with stack space for some 25,000 to 50,000 volumes, possibly in the Manhattan Buildings, for use in sorting the books and documents which have not yet been absorbed and which are in considerable measure kept in boxes in storage warehouses.

Document Indexes. The urgent need for current subject indexes to the United Nations and Specialized Agency documents was impressed upon me most emphatically during my visit to London, Geneva and Paris. The need is felt by DPI information centers, the Geneva Library, our Assembly Library, librarians of Specialized Agencies, many members of the Secretariat, and by librarians and other users of our documents. I am convinced that many man hours are now wasted by such agencies and people because we fail to do the job thoroughly and promptly at Lake Success.

I am glad to report that the Checklists and Indexes of documents previously issued are expected to be in print some time in 1949. It is estimated, or perhaps more accurately it is hoped, that these Checklists and Indexes by session can be kept fairly well up to date in the future unless the output of documents increases.

We hope to launch early in 1949 a weekly subject index to documents and publications issued by the United Nations and the Specialized Agencies. This undertaking will require special funds and special staff. It appears to us, however, that the demand is so great that means for launching and carrying on the enterprise must be found. In order to avoid misunderstanding, it should be stated emphatically that the weekly index as we propose it will not have the completeness or the accuracy of the Checklists and Indexes; what we are going to try to do is to prepare a practical working tool for all who need to use United Nations and Specialized Agency documents and publications. It should perhaps also be stated that the items included in any weeks issue of the new index will be those which have actually been received by the Documents Index Unit and the Division of Library Services. Obviously the documents will be listed promptly only if they are promptly received. Many questions, difficulties and problems have already arisen. We shall probably make many mistakes. Your criticisms will be welcomed as a means toward gradual improvement.

Eventually we hope to shift to the Service to Readers Unit of the Library many document reference questions which must now be answered by the Documents Index Unit, thus freeing the indexers to prepare and publish indexes. Many problems must be solved before this hope can be realized.

Depository Libraries. The designation of Depository Libraries and the arrangement of all exchanges of United Nations publications is the responsibility of the United Nations Headquarters Library Services, by formal action of the Publications Board. (Annex III of Paper no. 188 entitled "Principles of Policy for Designation of Depository Libraries and Exchange of Publications.")

We are authorized to establish:

One depository library in each member country.

Not more than 50 other depositories in member countries.

One depository in each non-member country in which it is impossible to arrange for satisfactory exchange relations.

Not more than 15 depository libraries in non-metropolitan territories.

Any parliamentary library may become a depository if it requests that privilege.

Under these regulations, we should eventually have approximately 140 or 150 depository libraries throughout the world. The number now in operation is only a fraction of that total.

Delays have been due, in part, to the inability of the Division of Library Services to get adequate information on which to make decisions, to our inability to get out the letters as soon as the decisions were made, and particularly to the failure of libraries to decide whether they wish to become depositories.

Exchanges. The Publications Board regulations also state, "the arrangements of all exchanges of United Nations publications shall be the responsibility of the United Nations Headquarters Library Services". Under this regulation we are authorized to arrange exchanges of all or any unrestricted United Nations publications in return for publications issued or for Library Services rendered by the recipient. We are also authorized, at our discretion, to arrange exchanges of special categories of United Nations unrestricted publications and presumably documents, with recognized centers for the study of international affairs, even though the return for the materials to be exchanged be disproportionate.

We now estimate that the total of such exchanges may involve 50 or more additional institutions in the not too distant future. Twenty-six such institutions are already involved. In addition to these groups already enumerated, the Library now has exchange relations with approximately 130 institutions, societies and editorial boards whereby we receive their publications in return for United Nations documents in categories which they have chosen.

Until we know how many libraries throughout the world can justify receipt of United Nations publications and documents on an exchange basis or as centers for international study, it is impossible to estimate with accuracy the number of depositories we should designate in order to reach and serve all the countries of the world. It now appears, however, that the present pattern for designating depository libraries provides adequate coverage only in those small nations where much of the population and activity center in the capital city. In the large nations, where great numbers of the people live and where much research and educational work are carried on outside the capital city, the supply of documents is likely to prove inadequate.

The Division will recommend authorization of additional depositories if the situation appears to require such action.

It must unfortunately be admitted that investigations up to this time lead us to believe that in many of the minor countries there are no libraries sufficiently staffed and budgeted to handle the documents which are produced by the United Nations.

Libraries which become depositories are requested to give the United Nations an undertaking to keep the material properly classified and available to the general public, free of charge, at all reasonable hours. It is a foregone conclusion that some of the libraries which have accepted depository status will not be able to live up to this undertaking. It would appear, therefore, that when the original arrangements are completed, the Division of Library Services or some other agency of the United Nations should be prepared to follow through. We should collect information as to which libraries are doing a good job, which ones are doing a poor job or nothing at all. We should collect information as to how the documents are handled in various types of libraries and make that information available to others, together with any suggestions and advice which may grow out of our own experience in handling the United Nations documents. It may be hoped that the designation of a depository in 1948 or 1949 will not result in the continuation of that institution as a depository indefinitely unless it is prepared to make the documents available to the people who want them. Many revisions in the list of document depositories may have to be made during the first several years.

Distribution of United Nations Publications. The

Division of Library Services is not responsible for the general distribution of informational publications to the libraries of the world, but it is interested in seeing the widest and freest possible distribution. We are glad to endorse the comment of the International Advisory Committee of Library Experts that the libraries of the world constitute an effective channel for the dissemination of information about the United Nations and the Specialized Agencies, "and that the United Nations should take advantage of this channel by making available to libraries on a generous scale publications of the DPI in as many languages as possible."

The Geneva Library. It should perhaps be said once more that the Division of Library Services and the DPI have no intention of transferring the Geneva Library to Lake Success or New York, in whole or in part. We endorse the recommendations on this subject made by the International Advisory Committee of Library Experts. In brief these are that the Geneva Library be maintained on approximately its present level, primarily for service to the United Nations and the Specialized Agencies, secondarily for the scholars and students of Europe; and that it inaugurate a liberal policy of interlibrary loans.

After my visit to Geneva last summer, I prepared a memorandum to Breycha-Vauthier in which several recommendations are made. Two or three of them may be mentioned here.

Because the Library is rather far removed from the offices of the Secretariat, I am recommending that a small branch library be established in the Secretariat wing. If feasible, this might be a consolidation of the DPI Reference Center and of the collection maintained by the Economic and Social Council. Another recommendation which I am very eager to follow through is that there be arranged exchanges of staff members between the Geneva and the Headquarters libraries as soon as possible and as frequently as possible. The purpose would be gradually to develop common policy, programmes, and practices. I found in Geneva as I found here last May (and as still prevails here to a considerable extent) that many professional librarians are called upon to spend a large part of their time as typists. Out of the 20 library staff members in Geneva not a single one is rated as typist or stenographer. This situation should be corrected. The visit resulted in the development of further co-operation between the two libraries. We are now exchanging order lists, catalogue cards, and information of various sorts.

Building Planning. Officers of the Division have had several conferences with the architects who are now preparing preliminary sketches for remodelling and equipping the Manhattan Building for library purposes. We expect to have the use of five floors and two basements, beginning whenever the other buildings are completed, probably in 1950. Later, we expect to have use of the sixth and seventh floors which are now occupied by the Military Staff Committee.

The two basements will presumably be used primarily for storage, receiving room, etc. Plans have already been prepared for the erection of stacks in the sub-basement to be used permanently for sorting and storage. What is now the first floor will have light only on the 42nd Street side after the grading is completed. The tunnel from the Secretariat building will come in on this floor. We expect therefore to have here an information or receptionist counter which will also serve as a return loan desk.

The second floor as it is now (which will become the ground floor opening on the plaza) will house a general reading room; the third, a United Nations and League of Nations documents room; the fourth, special collections; the fifth, offices and work rooms.

On the second, third and fourth floors, present plans call for reading rooms on the north (overlooking the plaza) and on the east (overlooking the river). Stacks and work rooms will occupy the other sides.

Both the architects and the librarians involved believe that this building will provide adequate and excellent space and location for the Division of Library Services. A pneumatic tube will connect the Library with the Secretariat building for rapid delivery of books.

Contracts. We have made contracts with the Library of Congress and the New York Public Library which enable them to provide us with specialized bibliographical information at our request. Several projects have been assigned to the libraries; one or two will serve as illustrations. One assigned to the Library of Congress was a project for compiling brief lists of the basic reference books on each of the Latin American countries. We need such books from all countries. Another was concerned with the preparation of lists intended to supplement certain regional bibliographies already issued by the Library of Congress, with a view to bringing them up to date for our use. Still another entailed the checking of a bibliography on food and nutrition which had been prepared in the Social Affairs Department of the United Nations.

Bibliographies. By formal action of some official United Nations bodies, certain units of the Secretariat are called upon to carry on a very large number of big research projects. Frequently a bibliography is a first requisite; the research staff is often inadequate for this and other work, so the Library receives a request to prepare the bibliography. An example is a request for a relatively complete list of all publications giving statistics of transportation, communication and industry, in all countries, for the past ten or twelve years.

Obviously the Library has neither the staff nor the competence to perform such tasks without assistance. Our present policy is to try to find some way to make a small exploratory study in the field, from which it will be possible to estimate the size and requirements of the whole job. When that has been done (in very close co-operation with the re-search group concerned) it may become necessary for the Li-brary and the research group to report to the budgetary au-thorities that the job can be completed only if special funds are appropriated for personnel, travel and materials.

This is on the assumption that extensive bibliographies can best be prepared by subject specialists and librarians working together.

Research Section. Much of the work of the Section has of necessity been concentrated on the preparation of the 1947-48 Yearbook. There will be certain differences between this Yearbook and the last. Thus, it has been decided that it should not be self-sufficient but that references should be made to the first volume. It will be copiously documented. Further, it has been decided that the policy of using the re-ports of the different organs of the United Nations--Security Council, Economic and Social Council, and Trusteeship Coun-cil--should not be followed, but that a better balance would be achieved if space were given to the views and proposals made in the Economic and Social Council and Trusteeship Council. This has involved dealing with all the documents of these organs during the period under review--about twice as much work as last year--which has meant that the Section has had to curtail its other activities. It is hoped, however, that the book will be ready in January, or, at the latest, in February, and that it will be in some respects an improvement on last year's book.

During 1948 this Section has produced fifteen Background Papers with two addenda; four series of Questions and Answers: on the Security Council, The U.N. Appeal for Children, the Economic and Social Council, and "U.N. and You" (for United Nations Day); four papers in the Outline Series; a six-monthly Chronology of Events and monthly series of anniversaries; and two miscellaneous papers: "Aims of the U.N." and "Structure of the U.N." It has compiled two publications: a new edition of "Basic Facts" and "Everyman's United Nations" (a new edition of the Guide for Lecturers and Teachers). It has also from time to time assisted other sections of the office by providing material, checking manuscripts, etc., and is at present engaged in producing its yearly batch of articles for encyclopedias.

Opinion Survey Section. Increasing interest in world opinion with regard to U.N. activities is evidenced by the growing demands for information supplementary to the regular Weekly Survey of Opinion.

During the Paris session of the General Assembly, all U.N. Information Centers were called upon to cable daily summaries of opinion to Paris; summaries of U.S. and Canadian comment were prepared in the Lake Success unit and transmitted via teletype.

At the request of the Secretary-General's office, a summary of U.S. and Canadian comment and coverage was sent to Mr. Lie in Oslo and Mr. Cordier in Paris during the four weeks prior to the opening of the Assembly. A very recent request from the same office for special material relating to opinion regarding the handling by the Organization of the refugee problem in Palestine is being met.

Special requests have been made by: the Legal Department for a daily summary of comment in regard to charges that spies were entering the U.S. through the U.N.; the Department of Economic Affairs for a continuation of the special survey on international trade and tariffs for the Interim Committee of the ITO; the Palestine Commission for daily summaries during the special Assembly on Palestine. All these requests were met.

The public, in spite of our fixed policy against promoting distribution of the survey, has shown interest in world opinion through many requests for complete sets of back issues of the Survey on the part of universities, libraries, individual students, the press and non-governmental organizations. Women United for United Nations considers the need for such information so important that it is taking active steps to organize a volunteer clipping of editorial opinion for our use.

Special material is being sent to the Committee of Good Offices for Indonesia and the Commission for India and Pakistan. The Department of Social Affairs has expressed interest in public reaction to the Assembly's approval of the Universal Declaration of Human Rights.

Internships and Exchanges. Several units of the Division of Library Services have shared in the internship programme which is carried on by the Training Division of the United Nations. We shall hope to be included in the plans for the International Center for Training in Public Administration which have recently had preliminary approval in Paris.

The Division offers such unusual opportunities for work experience that, in our opinion, it should be enabled to inaugurate and maintain an internship and exchange programme for the particular benefit of librarians.

We are convinced that if funds can be found it will be desirable to have at least twelve librarians, mostly from countries other than the United States, work in the Division for about six months every year. They should be young graduate librarians who have or expect to have library positions in their own countries. While here they will be given experience in various kinds of library work including the handling and indexing of United Nations documents. When they return to their home countries they will have a reasonably good knowledge of the United Nations, its documents and its library services. The Division would gain from having them, not only additional man-hours of work, but the stimulation which would come from having always in the Library a group of young librarians from several parts of the world.

Exchanges also offer numerous opportunities. We would give top priority to exchanges between Geneva and Headquarters. Next would come exchanges between Headquarters or Geneva on the one hand, and the Specialized

Agencies on the other.   Not too far down the list would be
exchanges with depository libraries.

Information Centers.   I have now visited DPI Information centers in Washington, London, Geneva and Paris.   I
have also attended a meeting with the directors of several
of the Information Centers.   From these observations and
discussions I am convinced that the library service in those
centers is important.   In fact, one Director stated that his
little library was the heart of his operations.   Primarily
these libraries are document reference centers, dealing with
United Nations and Specialized Agency materials.   Some also
have a modest selection of reference materials.   They are
called upon to answer all sorts of questions related to the
United Nations and Specialized Agencies and their work.   At
this time the Library Division has no direct relation to the
operation of these libraries.   It would not be able to assume
any responsibility if it were asked.   It is possible, however,
that some time in the future the Library can at least give
over-all advisory service and assist in the preparation of
brief lists of books for acquisition by the Centers.   A specific suggestion from the directors with whom I talked in
Paris was that someone be made available to help organize
the libraries in the various Centers, a librarian who could
spend a month in each, helping to put the materials in shape
and to advise the acting librarian on various problems.   If
it ever became possible to put a trained librarian on the staff
of each of these Centers, many of the present difficulties
will find their solution naturally.

International Advisory Committee of Library Experts.
One of the most useful experiences of the year was the meeting of this Committee which was convened for ten days in
August to advise on library programme and policy.   Seven
distinguished librarians from seven countries accepted our
invitation.   One country which was asked to designate a librarian failed to reply.   At the meeting were also the librarians or other representatives of several of the Specialized
Agencies.   The meetings were extraordinarily productive as
indicated by the excellent report which has already been referred to in this communication.

Following the general meeting, there was a meeting
of the representatives of the Specialized Agencies and of the
Division.   A Co-ordinating Committee was formed and several recommendations were made for the mutual benefit of
the several organizations.

Budget--1949. The manning table, as approved, provides for 80 posts in the Division as compared with 68 in 1948. Several of these posts were available on a temporary basis during the latter part of 1948. The amount appropriated for books and equipment is $88,000--$20,000 less than the amount requested, and about $10,000 less than the amount available in 1948. The fund for contractual services is renewed at $20,000. The 1949 manning table for the Geneva Library remains the same as in 1948 with 20 posts. The Geneva Library book fund is $22,000, a slight increase over 1948. In addition the Geneva Library is now authorized to use for books and equipment a sum of $23,000 from the income of the Library Endowment Funds.

The Staff. The 80 posts include 27 assigned to the Document Index Unit, the Opinion Survey Section and the Research Section, leaving 53 for the Service to Readers, Acquisition and Cataloguing Units and the Director's office.

They represent 16 nationalities and speak 17 languages. All speak English; 24 speak French; 14 speak German, and 12 speak Spanish. From 1-6 speak Italian, Russian, Yiddish, Ukrainian, Slovakian, Finnish, Chinese, Czech, Portuguese, Dutch, Danish, Norwegian and Swedish. Reading ability covers also Serbian, Croatian, and Polish.

Bouquets and Brickbats. My associates tell me that an occasional complimentary remark is made about the Library Services and that the criticisms appear to be diminishing somewhat. But we are keeping our fingers crossed.

The catch is that a great many justifiable criticisms can be made. Our Checklists and Indexes should be issued promptly. A current subject index is a necessity. Cataloguing should be brought up to date. More attention must be given to Government documents than has been possible recently; departmental liaison library personnel should be slightly increased; more binding is needed; reading room space should be expanded. These and a dozen other criticisms will continue to be made until we have found the means to make these improvements. Some recommendations have been hinted at in this letter and will be formally presented to the appropriate officials from time to time.

We in the Division think that if, with your help, we can continue for two years to make such progress as we have made this year we shall have a reasonably good Library and Library Services when we move to Manhattan.

Appendix F

THE UNITED NATIONS LIBRARY*

Carl H. Milam

The headquarters Library of the United Nations now
has approximately 165,000 volumes; a temporarily usable
building on the permanent United Nations site; a staff of about
eight-five persons, half professional, half clerical, representing some twenty member nations, with a working facility
in more than thirty languages; and a definite library policy
which has been adopted by the General Assembly.

Before the San Francisco conference the United Nations
was served by the library of the United States Department of
State. At the conference the Library of Congress, with assistance from the New York branch of the United Nations Information Office and loans from other libraries, organized
and operated a special library in San Francisco. The Pre-
paratory Commission at its meeting in London had at its disposal a library comprising books on loan and a core collection which was the property of the Secretariat.

In the spring of 1946 a considerable part of this latter
collection was moved to the temporary headquarters at Hunter
College in New York City, where it was incorporated into a
library established in the Department of Conference and General Services of the Secretariat. This library was moved to
Lake Success along with the Secretariat in August, 1946. At
that time there was added to its book stock the collection of
publications, chiefly documents, belonging to the former Economic and Transit Division of the League of Nations, which
had served the members of the division working at Princeton
during the war years. A further substantial addition was made
when the library of the United Nations Relief and Rehabilitation Administration was acquired by the United Nations in the
spring of 1947.

*Reprinted by permission of the University of Chicago Press
from Library Quarterly 23,4 (October 1953), 267-80.

When the United Nations Information Office in New
York was disbanded, the books, documents, and periodicals
belonging to it were transferred to a reference center set up
in the Department of Public Information of the Secretariat.
This center functioned side by side with the United Nations
Library during the Hunter College days and later on at Lake
Success. In January, 1948, it became a part of the general
library.

Although the position of the Library was far from
clear at the time of the move to Lake Success, its role and
functions in the Secretariat were greatly strengthened when,
in August, 1946, by order of the secretary-general, on recommendation of the assistant secretary-general in charge of the
Department of Conference and General Services, the general
library was made responsible for all library acquisitions and
services. However, a considerable period of time elapsed
before the terms of this order were fully complied with.

Following a management survey of the Secretariat, of
which a library survey was a part, all library services under
whatever name (with minor exceptions) were set up as a Division of Library Services in the Department of Public Information. On January 1, 1949, the Library was again transferred.
This time it became an independent unit attached to the Executive Office of the secretary-general. Such a transfer had been
suggested in 1947, and the action was finally taken on the
recommendation of the Department of Administrative and Financial Services.

In late 1950 and early 1951, the Library was moved,
with the Secretariat, to the permanent site on East Forty-
second Street, New York.

LIBRARY POLICY

The Library began its existence, quite naturally, without any well-defined policy. But in the minds of many, especially of those members of the Secretariat and delegations
who had been connected with the League of Nations, the
League library offered a precedent worth following.

In April, 1947, after some inquiries by the American
Library Association and the librarian of Congress, the assistant secretary-general in charge of the Department of Conference and General Services solicited the advice of one

European and three American librarians. Planning for United
Nations buildings on the permanent site was then in its early
stages. The chief question put to the committee of consultants concerned space requirements for the Library. Obviously, no recommendations could be made on this subject
without some preliminary decisions as to the future size of
the collection and the nature of the services to be rendered.

After two days of observation and discussion, including
a meeting with the Permanent Advisory Commiteee on the Library (representing several departments of the Secretariat),
the committee made its report to the assistant secretary-
general of the Department of Conference and General Services.
It recommended, among other things, emphasis on reference
and bibliographical service rather than on accumulation and
preservation of a large collection; and a wing for the Library
attached to the proposed Secretariat building.

The committee also proposed that a competent librarian be engaged "to make a quick estimate of the quantities of
materials which will probably be needed in each important
subject field and geographical area"; and a library building
expert "to translate the requirements of the Library into a
building programme and a list of space requirements."
Prompt action was taken on these two proposals by engaging
Mr. Verner W. Clapp, of the Library of Congress, for the
former task and Mr. John E. Burchard, of the Massachusetts
Institute of Technology, for the latter.

Mr. Clapp interviewed many members of the Secretariat as to their needs and found that there existed a hope
"that all pertinent materials will be available in the particular
library which is prepared for the particular worker's use
... that the Library will be self-contained." In his report
of May 3, 1947, he nevertheless called attention to the large
library collections which are available in and near New York
City and recommended extensive use of interlibrary loans and
avoidance of unnecessary duplication, especially of older materials. He did not specifically recommend a maximum size
for the collection but did state that, on the basis of his estimates, "stack space for 500,000 volumes should provide room
for growth for 10 to 20 years, without weeding" and that a
1,000,000-volume stack would meet the needs for from nine-
teen to thirty-eight years without weeding. This report included many other important recommendations, especially
concerning categories and quantities of library materials likely
to be needed.

Mr. Burchard's report was made on May 5, 1947.
He had apparently been asked to prepare his analysis of space
requirements on the assumption that storage for 1,500,000
volumes would be required. He complied with this request.
But he felt strongly that the figure was much too high, in
view of the availability of the vast library resources of the
New York area. He therefore presented also his estimates
based on a maximum of 500,000 volumes.

The concept of a relatively small working library and
extensive use of the resources of other libraries met with
the approval of policy-making officials of the Secretariat. In
the summer of 1948 a working policy based on that concept
was informally established by the Division of Library Services
and the Department of Public Information, of which it was a
part.

One further step was considered necessary before a
formal statement of policy could be submitted to the General
Assembly for approval. That was to get the advice of an
international committee of library experts. Consequently, the
assistant secretary-general of the Department of Public Infor-
mation invited seven distinguished librarians to meet at Lake
Success for several days in August, 1948. They were: Mr.
Verner W. Clapp, Library of Congress, United States; Mr.
F. C. Francis, British Museum, United Kingdom; Mlle
Yvonne Oddon, Musée de l'Homme, France; Mr. Abdel Moneim
M. Omar, Egyptian National Library, Egypt; Mr. S. R. Ran-
ganathan, Delhi University, India; Mr. Jorge Ugarte-Vial,
Biblioteca del Congreso nacional, Chile; and Mr. Ewang Tsing
Wu, National Library of Peiping, China. (Mr. Clapp and
Mr. Ugarte-Vial substituted for Dr. Luther Evans and Dr.
Jorge Basadre, who were ill; Mlle Oddon for M. Julien Cain,
who was unable to leave France at that time.) Mr. Francis
was elected chairman; Mr. Clapp, vice-chairman. Representatives of the libraries of several specialized agencies sat
with the committee and participated in the discussions. Several American librarians attended one or more sessions as
informal consultants.

The committee was outstanding for its earnest, con-
scientious, frank, and, in the end, harmonious work on the
library problem. Often the discussions went on far into the
night after the formal meeting adjourned, with the result that
the members returned in the morning with their differences
resolved. The final report was unanimously adopted.

In anticipation of the committee meeting the Library
staff had prepared, as is the United Nations' practice, three
"working papers" on history, current practice, problems, and
recommendations and, of course, the agenda for each session.
The working papers were on (1) general library policy; (2)
distribution and use of United Nations documents and departmental publications (the Library is responsible for establish-
ing depository libraries, for exchanges, and for document
indexing; it is not responsible for general distribution of
United Nations documents); and (3) special considerations, including sections on the Geneva library; libraries of the specialized agencies; and internships, fellowships, and exchanges
involving United Nations library services. Subcommittees
corresponding to these three areas were appointed.

The committee's report appeared in English and French
as document A/C.5/222, August 30, 1948, entitled <u>Interna-
tional Advisory Committee of Library Experts: Report of
Session held at Lake Success, New York, 2-9 August 1948</u>:
also in a pamphlet in each of the two languages, entitled
<u>United Nations Library Services</u> and <u>Services de la Biblio-
thèque</u>. (All of these items are now out of print.)

As far as possible, the Division of Library Services
carried out the recommendations of this committee, and the
committee report was used as the basis for the official policy
statement which was adopted by the General Assembly in December, 1949.* That statement is consistent with the recommendations of the 1947 Committee of Consultants, of Mr.
Clapp, and of Mr. Burchard. Perhaps the spirit and purpose
are best shown by a sentence from paragraph 8: "... the
emphasis will be on service and immediate usefulness, not
on accumulation and preservation."

THE COLLECTIONS

In building up the Library's resources, the first criterion is current usefulness. Collections on every subject
chosen for inclusion must, if possible, be balanced geograph-
ically and linguistically. On issues of debate all points of
view should be represented. With minor exceptions, the size
of the collection on any subject is adjusted to the probable
intensity and duration of the problem or research project

---

*<u>Official Records of the General Assembly</u> (Fourth Sess.,
Fifth Committee, Annex); Vol. I, agenda item 39.

which created the need for it and the permanent value as
continuously useful material.

The 1947 Committee of Consultants foresaw the need
for complete files of documents of the United Nations and
specialized agencies; collections of "documents, periodicals,
pamphlets, newspapers and clippings, books, processed reports and studies, maps, pictures, sound records, films,
etc., on each member State, other nations, and all subjects
with which the United Nations deals," such as "treaties, government, law, military affairs, atomic energy, economics,
finance, transportation, communication, agriculture,* statistics, health,* human rights, social welfare, displaced persons, etc."

In 1949 the reference staff compiled a list of "Subjects
of Interest to the United Nations Library" as a guide to book
selection. It comprised some 250 topics, arranged under the
following main subjects: history; political science, including
international relations; international and national law; arma-
ments; atomic energy; trusteeship and nonself-governing territories; economics, transport, and communications; social
problems; science and technology; geography; general works.

A few subheadings selected more or less at random
will suggest the wide range of materials actually needed.
Under history, "Contemporary political, economic, and social
conditions in the various countries of the world." Under economics, transport and communications, statistics in all kinds
of publications and from all countries on "Population, housing,
health, insurance, criminality, migration, manpower, employment, agricultural and livestock production, industrial production indexes; production in mining and quarrying, manufactur-
ing, construction, electricity and gas, transport (railroad,
road, ocean and air), communications (postal, telegraph and
broadcast); internal and external trade, balance of payments,
wages and prices, currency, banking and stock exchange
operations, national income and public finance."

Under social problems: "Social services: social welfare administration; international fellowships; the training of
social welfare staff; the needs of the underdeveloped countries
for these services."

Under general works: "Unilingual dictionaries:

---

*These subjects are of primary concern to F.A.O. and W.H.O.

authoritative ones in all languages. New dictionaries of any of the official languages (English, French, Spanish, Russian, Chinese) which contribute something not obtainable elsewhere. Etymological dictionaries and dictionaries of synonyms and antonyms, etc., of the official languages; dictionaries of the terminologies of any of the special subjects recorded elsewhere in this list, and terminological dictionaries of scientific and technical subjects."

This list of topics is under constant revision as new research projects are undertaken and the work of the organization is broadened.

The Library's holdings are estimated at about 165,000 volumes, 45,000 maps, 2,750 reels of microfilms, together with constantly fluctuating collections of unbound magazines, government documents, newspapers, pamphlets, and clippings. They fall into several categories.

United Nations and specialized agencies documents and publications. --In these fields the Library's goal is completeness, in all languages, with sufficient copies for both reference and circulation. Books about these organizations are also systematically collected.

The number of documents and publications issued by the United Nations from 1945 through 1952 is estimated at more than 150,000. These range in size from one page to more than a thousand pages. The Library now has about 11,000 volumes of these documents and publications on its shelves in bound form, and the binding is being gradually completed so that all will be permanently preserved. At the 1952 rate of publication the annual intake is estimated at 65,000 pieces, including needed duplicates.

The specialized agencies are also prolific in output, with an estimated annual production of about 18,000 pieces. Bound volumes of these documents on the Library shelves now number nearly 10,000.

League of Nations documents and publications. --Here also the goal is a complete collection of official documents and publications, together with all important books about the League and about peace movements during the period between the two world wars. The gift to the United Nations by the Woodrow Wilson Foundation in 1950 of its excellent library, comprising some 16,500 volumes, greatly strengthened the

Library's holdings of League materials. The books and documents by and about the League already in the United Nations
Library--about 4,000 volumes--were combined with those received from the foundation to create what may possibly be
the most complete collection of League documents outside
Geneva. It is now called the Woodrow Wilson Memorial Library. The excellent catalog of League publications, which
had been prepared by the Woodrow Wilson Foundation, with
financial assistance from the Rockefeller Foundation, was
transferred with the books and documents and adds greatly to
the usefulness of this library. Materials about the League
and its work continue to be acquired.

General reference. --The collection is strong in bibliographical works, biographical dictionaries, handbooks of political, economic, and social information, compilations of laws
and treaties, general and special encyclopedias, and dictionaries. In these categories the best and most useful works
from all countries in all languages are sought.

Government documents. --Probably no part of the Library collection reveals as well as that comprising government documents the extent and variety of the research work
being carried on continuously by the United Nations. More
than one hundred categories are now solicited from member
governments, trust and nonself-governing territories, and non-
member nations. These categories range from constitutions
and laws to foreign affairs, financial reports, and statistics
of all kinds; from transportation, natural resources, and industrial production to narcotics, human rights, and child welfare. Official gazettes are of primary importance, and the
Library's holdings are extensive.

Periodicals. --The Library now receives about 200
newspaper and 2,000 magazine titles, not including government serials. Many are sent directly to the four departmental libraries for circulation to staff members of the departments. Others are routed to individuals or units of the
Secretariat. About 25 newspapers and 100 magazines are
displayed in the general periodical room. Some periodicals
are discarded after a few months; others are retained for
varying periods; about 375 titles are regularly bound for long-
time service.

Maps. --The map collection consists of some 45,000
maps and about 750 atlases, gazetteers, guides, and other
cartographic reference books; also national flags and seals

from most countries. About 3,000 items are now added annually. This is one unit of the Library which illustrates the
difficulty of limiting the size of its holdings; for example,
maps of a region which appear useless one day may be in
great demand a few days later because that region has become an area of tension or conflict.

TABLE 1

	Pieces	Per Cent
Books	10,000	3.6
Periodicals.	64,000	23.1
Documents of national governments . .	101,847	36.7
Maps	6,000	2.2
United Nations and specialized agency issuances	95,000	34.4
Total	276,847	100.0

Table 1 shows acquisitions during 1951, according to
a recent report prepared by Mr. Verner W. Clapp.

ADMINISTRATIVE ORGANIZATION

The Library operates as an independent unit attached
to the Executive Office of the secretary-general. Major policy decisions are approved by that office, but the Library
handles its own administrative problems. Relations with the
Personnel and Budget Bureaus are direct, and the Library
must make its own case before the Advisory Committee on
Administrative and Budgetary Questions and before the General Assembly's Fifth Committee (Budgets and Administration).

The Library organization consists of the director's office, including the executive officer and secretarial assistants;
the Reference and Documentation Section, including a Service
to Readers Unit and a Departmental Libraries Unit; and the
Processing Section, with Acquisition, Cataloguing, and Documents Index Units.

LIBRARY SERVICES

The nature of the services had been indicated by the
paragraphs on policy and collections.

The Library exists primarily to provide materials, information, and services needed by the delegations, Secretariat, and other official groups in the performance of their duties. The needs may be said to arise in three ways:

1. Issues before the General Assembly and Councils and tasks assigned to commissions and committees. Some political issues, like the Korean crisis, arise almost overnight. The Library must be prepared to supply on a few hours' notice, from its own collections or from other libraries, the essential geographical, political, economic, and social data on any new area of tension. Other problems, such as technical assistance to underdeveloped countries, come gradually into prominence and permit the Library to assemble and make available a few basic materials in orderly fashion. Still others represent subjects of permanent interest, such as population and economic development.

2. The research and publication projects undertaken by the Secretariat. As this is written, many scores of major research projects are in progress. They are on such varied subjects as housing, town and country planning, child welfare laws of all countries, extra-territorial waters, public finance statistics, and narcotic drugs. The Catalogue of Economics and Social Projects, issued by the Department of Economic Affairs in 1951, listed 349 studies in these fields alone. There are always in process, too, a considerable number of minor studies on topics likely to be of interest in the near future. They may be on the world's supply of phosphates, international cartels, or higher education in a trusteeship area. Publication projects are of two kinds, the single report, as, for example, on the nationality of married women or agricultural requisites in Latin America; or a periodical publication, such as the Monthly Bulletin of Statistics.

3. Administrative and legal problems which inevitably arise in connection with the operation of the organization. Some of these involve the use of books on administration, national financial procedures, civil service, etc. Others require League of Nations documents (for precedents), legal texts, codes, court reports, and treaties.

The direct responsibility for meeting these needs "with the greatest possible speed, convenience, and economy" rests on the Service to Readers and Departmental Libraries units operating as the Reference and Documentation Section, with the co-operation of the acquisition, cataloging, and indexing services of the Processing Section.

The chief of the Service to Readers Unit supervises the main reference room, the periodical room, the United Nations and Specialized Agencies Documents Collection, the Woodrow Wilson Memorial Library, the map collection, and the stacks.

The main reference room provides service from the general reference collection: government documents, pamphlets, clippings, microfilms, and the main book collection. One of the five professional staff members assigned to this service devotes a large part of his time to the indexing of periodical articles on the United Nations and the specialized agencies. Another gives special attention to the filing of pamphlets and bibliographies.

As in all reference collections, the questions range from the very simple to the very complex, the time consumed in answering them varying from a few minutes to several days. New projects often require comprehensive surveys of the Library's holdings in a special field, the preparation of bibliographies and reading lists, and a search for materials in other libraries. Most inquirers expect rapid service because they are meeting deadlines. All need the latest and most authentic information. Two or more sources must be checked and compared on controversial matters. Publications in more than one language are often required. The members of the reference staff possess linguistic abilities which enable them to handle queries in several languages.

Reference work on United Nations and specialized agencies documents is a part of the Service to Readers Unit, now operated on a separate floor with a staff of two professionals and two subprofessionals. Questions relate to all the activities and documents of all these organizations.

The Woodrow Wilson Memorial Library occupies another floor, supplying documents and information about all aspects of the League of Nations, the publications of the International Labor Organization from 1919 to 1945, and the work of the Permanent Court of International Justice.

The periodical room, adjacent to the main reference room, is the central service point for all magazines and newspapers. Current titles are on display; recent issues

are in adjoining stacks; the bound volumes, though housed
elsewhere, are serviced by the attendant in this room.

The map collection, under the care of a trained geog-
rapher, receives a wide variety of inquiries, ranging from
the simple identification of a place name to problems which
necessitate intensive area studies.

Departmental libraries. --When the secretary-general
in 1946 made the general library responsible for all library
acquisitions and services, six departments had assembled
their own collections. A reference service was maintained
by the Department of Public Information, largely for the use
of newspaper correspondents and radio broadcasters. The
Departments of Security Council Affairs, Economic Affairs,
Social Affairs, Trusteeship and Information from Non-Self-
governing Territories, and Legal Affairs also had their libraries.

The materials and staff of the reference service of the
Department of Public Information became a part of the general library in 1948, when the latter was set up as a Division of Library Services in that department. When the new
Secretariat building was occupied, the number of departmental
libraries was reduced to four, by consolidation of the two
branches serving economic affairs and social affairs. Each
of the four now occupies a small space in the Secretariat
building.

The need for these branches is sometimes questioned
by individual members of some delegations. But the Library
staff and the departments concerned believe their maintenance
to be justified in the interest of fast and convenient service
to the research workers and also as a means of having one
member of the Library staff within each of the substantive
departments who makes it his business to know almost from
hour to hour what new projects are contemplated and to act
as liaison between the departments and the Library.

The official policy statement says: "The maintenance
by the Library of branches within the departments of the Secretariat is a necessity, but these branches will be kept small
and will contain only the most needed reference materials....
The collections are integral parts of the Library; the personnel are members of the Library's staff." The departmental
library buildings [sic, i.e. collections] are not static; little-
used materials are returned to the main Library.

Circulation. --The Library has a liberal lending policy.
Nearly all books and documents may be borrowed by members
of the delegations and the Secretariat. Exceptions are a few
basic reference books and certain rare items, such as are
found in the Woodrow Wilson Memorial Library. Because of
the dispersal of the collections, loans are made from six
service points in the main Library: the central loan desk;
the periodical room; the United Nations and Specialized Agencies collection; the Woodrow Wilson Memorial Library, the
reference room (for reference books), and the map collection.
Loans are also made by the departmental libraries. More
than 90,000 pieces are circulated annually. The routing of
periodicals is a function of the serials checking desk and also
of departmental libraries. To meet the demand for material
not in its own collection, the Library borrows annually about
7,000 volumes from other libraries, mostly in the New York
area.

In spite of the convenience of the departmental libraries
and the excellent service given by them and the main Library,
the demands for books to be used in individual offices are
heavy. There are several reasons for this. One is the considerable time required to go from an office in the Secretariat building to the Library building. Other reasons are that
some officials consider it necessary to have their associates
always available for immediate consultation and, in the interest of security, want them to work in private. Similar considerations limit visits by members of the Secretariat to other
libraries.

Service to the public. --For budgetary and other reasons
the Library is not available to the general public. Its primary function, of course, is to serve the Secretariat and
other official groups of the organization. However, its services are also available to the specialized agencies, accredited
representatives of mass media of communication, international
governmental organizations and affiliated nongovernmental organizations, and--within certain limits--to educational institutions, scholars, and writers. It is not anticipated that any
serious research worker will ever be excluded if he needs
access to United Nations and League of Nations materials
which are not elsewhere available.

ACQUISITION

The Acquisition Unit procures books, periodicals,

government documents, and maps; printed, mimeographed,
offset, photostated or microfilmed; by exchange, gift, or purchase. It conducts the correspondence, checks the receipt,
and keeps the records necessary to undertake and complete
such transactions. It selects for possible discard incoming
materials of doubtful usefulness and refers them for decision
to the Reference and Documentation Section. It forwards
promptly to the Catalogue Unit or other parts of the Library
the materials which are to be retained.

Books are usually purchased through dealers, preferably in the country of publication. The need for speed causes
many exceptions. Prices and discounts are watched carefully,
but quick acquisition is frequently more important than the
saving of a few cents or a few dollars.

Of the private organizations and institutions with which
the Library has gift and exchange relations, two-thirds send
their material as outright gifts and one-third have exchange
arrangements. Libraries designated as depositories in the
category of international study centers are all potential sources
of exchange materials.

The acquisition of documents is one of the most important functions of the Acquisition Unit. Careful selectivity is
exercised, in order not to receive unwanted titles. At the
present time the publications of fifty-two member governments,
twenty nonmember governments, and seventy trust territories
and nonself-governing territories are received. This material
comes to the Library by way of delegations, and from issuing
bodies, United Nations information centers, and, in the case
of United States government publications, through the services
of a part-time document expediter in Washington, employed by
the Library of Congress under contractual funds.

At the serial checking desk, clerical assistants record
on visible indexes the receipt of all magazines, newspapers,
annuals, and government serials, mark the items for routing,
and answer telephone inquiries covering the Library's holdings
in this field. This is the only place in the Library where a
complete record of a current serial title can be found.

The Acquisition Unit places orders and gift requests
for materials needed by missions, commissions, information
centers, and training centers in many parts of the world.
The funds for these purchases are carried on budgets other
than that of the Library, but the work, which in late years

has amounted to more than one-third of the total load, is
largely absorbed by the unit.

It is also responsible for maintaining--and this is from
Library book funds--a supply of desk reference books which
are needed by members of the Secretariat in their offices.

Although binding is a responsibility primarily of the
Catalogue Unit, the Acquisition Unit keeps the financial records because binding funds are set up in the budget as a part
of book funds.

CATALOGING

As in many other libraries, the catalogers in the
United Nations Library during the first few years were unable
to keep pace with the incoming material. By 1948 the arrears, for a small library, were disproportionately large.
An elaborate system of priorities had been established to assure prompt handling of most urgently needed items. However, it was often found necessary to meet demands by sending books on with only the briefest of records to indicate
their location. The departmental libraries were almost
wholly uncataloged.

For the solution of this problem, the United Nations is
indebted largely to the Harvard University Library. In 1949,
Mr. Andrew D. Osborn, its assistant librarian, came on loan
to the United Nations Library as acting chief of the Processing Section. He served in this capacity for a total of three
months. Later, upon his return to Cambridge, Miss Susan
Haskins, of Harvard, served as acting chief of the Catalogue
Unit for nine months. Mr. Osborn returned at frequent intervals as consultant. During these twelve months the cataloging procedures were simplified and streamlined.

All important decisions were made after staff conferences, which were attended not only by catalogers but also
by representatives of all Library units. Some of the decisions were that the United Nations Library is to be recognized as a special library; that the records must be accurate
but not necessarily complete bibliographically; that emphasis
must be on speed; that subject headings must be in the ter-
minology which the United Nations uses; that every item, even
purchased materials, must be challenged as to its usefulness
and referred to the reference staff for approval, if of doubtful

value; that self-cataloging methods be used whenever applic-
able; that there be no unnecessary duplication of records
available elsewhere in the Library; that the card catalog be
divided into two parts, author and subject. Adherence to
these policies and procedures has served to keep any appre-
ciable backlog of uncataloged material from accumulating.

DOCUMENT INDEXING

The Documents Index Unit was created in the early
days of the organization as a part of the Bureau of Documents
to provide information to delegations, the Secretariat, and
the press on United Nations documents. Some check lists
and indexes were prepared, but reference service was em-
phasized. No comprehensive scheme for the bibliographical
control of all items issued was possible until the publication
program itself was stabilized.

In 1947 three conferences were held with librarians
and other representatives of research institutions in the
United States, and it was decided to issue the Check List of
United Nations Documents in several parts, one for each of
the principal organs, which are the General Assembly, the
Security Council, the Economic and Social Council, the Trusteeship Council, the International Court of Justice, and the
Secretariat. Three indexers were made available to the unit
through special funds provided for one year by the Carnegie
Endowment for International Peace. (In 1948 the unit became
a part of the Division of Library Services.) The task proved
to be more burdensome than had been estimated, and the arrears were accumulating.

In 1949 the Library requested a survey by the Inspection Service of the Secretariat. Mr. Roy Eastin, assistant
superintendent of documents for the United States, and Mr.
Jerome K. Wilcox, librarian of City College, New York, were
invited as consultants. Other librarians and research workers
who make extensive use of United Nations documents gave
their advice. The Library finally recommended a United Nations Documents Index, which would list and index all unrestricted documents and publications received during one month
from the United Nations and the specialized agencies. The
new monthly was launched in January, 1950. The subject index is cumulated annually. Several of the specialized agencies
currently prepare index cards for their own publications for
inclusion in the United Nations Documents Index.

Publication of the check lists by organs for 1946-49 is nearing completion.

In 1951 the reference functions were detached from the Documents Index Unit to become part of the Service to Readers Unit. The unit and its indexing functions were transferred to the Processing Section.

In addition to the preparation of the United Nations Documents Index and completing the check list, the unit indexes the United Nations Treaty Series; indexes daily the documents of the General Assembly, the Security Council, the Economic and Social Council, and the Trusteeship Council; publishes Disposition of Agenda Items; prepares cumulative indexes to resolutions and decisions of the General Assembly, Economic and Social Council, and Trusteeship Council; and gives advice on indexing problems to other units of the Secretariat.

DOCUMENT DEPOSITORIES

The Acquisition, Catalogue, and Documents Index units constitute the Processing Section. The chief of that section is responsible also for maintaining relations with depository libraries for United Nations documents and international study centers, which likewise receive this material. Under a directive from the Publications Board, a committee of the Secretariat, the director of the Library designates the depositories. The number of libraries in all these categories is now 185, in seventy-six countries.

The maintenance of a system of depository libraries is primarily for the purpose of making detailed information about the organization easily available to government officials, students, scholars, and writers all over the world. Mere designation and delivery of the documents do not necessarily achieve the desired result. The United Nations Library is conscious of its responsibility toward the depositories to assist them whenever possible with advice on the best means of organizing and maintaining their collections. It seeks to do this by keeping in close contact with United Nations information centers, whose officers visit depositories within the geographic areas which they serve, by issuing simple manuals of organization, and by publishing pertinent articles in library periodicals.

With certain exceptions, nondepository libraries are

expected to buy such publications and documents as they need.
In general, this arrangement is reasonably satisfactory. But
a much wider distribution of certain materials, especially to
schools and colleges is, in the opinion of many, desirable.

THE LIBRARY BUILDING

On the advice of the library consultants and architects,
it was decided in 1947 that the Library should not be housed
in the Secretariat building but in a semi-independent wing. A
possible need to expand this unit later was the primary reason.

As no such wing has been erected, the Library is temporarily housed in a building which was on the permanent site
when it was acquired. It has been adapted to library uses to
some extent, is well lighted and ventilated, is not far from
the Secretariat building, and is connected with it by a tunnel
and a pneumatic tube. But it has many disadvantages. The
floors were not constructed to carry a heavy load; a disproportionately large amount of space is given over to elevators,
stairways, and toilets; the location of these facilities in the
center of the building creates problems of supervision and re-
sults in inefficient use of space; and the total book-storage
capacity is much less than it should be.

It has now been decided that a permanent library building must be constructed as soon as the necessary funds can
be found. Preliminary sketches are in preparation, based on
an anticipated maximum collection of 400,000 volumes, with
generous provision for readers, especially in private studies.

BUDGETS

A recent study revealed that the United Nations is
spending about 2 per cent of its total Secretariat budget for
the Library, whereas the library costs of several other institutions with similar research interests run from 2.85 to 6.63
per cent of the total institutional budget.

The budget is prepared in successive drafts by staff
members at the administrative level, reviewed by the director,
discussed at staff conferences, and approved by the director.
A representative of the Bureau of Finance then reviews the
proposals, makes suggestions to bring them into line with

the secretary-general's policy for the year, and makes his recommendations to the chief of his bureau.

The text as approved is incorporated in the estimates of the whole Secretariat and issued as a United Nations document. This document is scrutinized with great care by the Advisory Committee on Administrative and Budgetary Questions, an independent committee of nine members from nine countries who are appointed as individuals qualifying as experts in administration and finance. The director of the Library has a hearing before this committee and is given an opportunity to defend any items which may be challenged. At the end of its sittings the committee publishes a report to the General Assembly, which likewise appears as an official document. It contains criticisms and specific recommendations.

The budgets then go to the Fifth Committee of the General Assembly (Budget and Administration), together with the advisory committee's report and any supplementary statements from the secretary-general. This is a committee of sixty members, each of whom represents a member country officially. Again the director of the Library is given a chance to answer questions.

Approval of budgets by this committee is followed by a more or less perfunctory approval by the General Assembly.

LIBRARY COMMITTEE

From the early days there has been an advisory committee on the Library. At first, it represented only the five substantive departments of the Secretariat; now it represents all departments and the Executive Office of the secretary-general. Formerly it met on the call of the assistant secretary-general in charge of the department of which the Library was a part, and he presided as chairman. Now it meets on the call of the Library director, who serves as chairman. It is purely advisory, but it has been helpful in some major policy decisions.

PUBLICATIONS

In addition to many document indexes already referred to, the Library issues a monthly list of "New Publications in the United Nations Headquarters Library," occasional numbers of a "Selected List of Periodical Articles in the United Nations Headquarters Library," and (sometimes in co-operation with other units of the Secretariat) numerous other bibliographical items. Three of the departmental libraries regularly issue lists of recently acquired documents.

THE LIBRARY STAFF

The staff is recruited internationally. The Charter states: "The paramount consideration in the employment of the staff ... shall be the necessity of securing the highest standards of efficiency, competence, and integrity. Due regard shall be paid to the importance of recruiting the staff on as wide a geographical basis as possible." In actual practice, the policy of the organization is to keep the professional personnel in the Secretariat balanced among member countries. The quotas set are related to each member country's financial contribution. They are not absolutely controlling but serve as a guide. These quotas apply, not to a unit like the Library, but to the Secretariat as a whole.

The Library is conscious of its need for representatives from many countries. It must have people with facility in the language and knowledge of the national or regional bibliography of many areas. All members must speak English. In most units the Library needs French, Spanish, German, the Slavic languages, and Chinese.

But languages and knowledge of a regional bibliography are not all. Good librarianship, good personality, lack of racial and national prejudices, a concept of United Nations ideals, and the ability to work with many people are also necessary.

Recruiting and employment are functions of the Bureau of Personnel. Suggestions from the Library are welcomed. The world-wide search for competent and available librarians, preferably from under-represented countries, sometimes causes serious delays in filling vacant posts. One individual in the bureau is assigned to work with the Library. In addition to recruiting and employment, he serves also as friend and counselor to any employee who chooses to consult him about his individual problems.

The present Library staff is competent by any standard; its morale is high; its production good; its teamwork excellent.

THE GENEVA LIBRARY

The former League of Nations Library in Geneva is now the Geneva Library of the United Nations. It has a collection of more than 400,000 volumes and a staff of twenty-three. It serves the United Nations Secretariat of approximately 600 in Geneva, the Economic Commission for Europe, the United Nations conferences held in Geneva, the specialized agencies in Geneva, and students and scholars. The Library Policy Statement calls for a continuation of the Library at approximately its present levels, and for no transfer of materials (other than duplicates or discards) to New York.

Administratively the Geneva Library is responsible to the director of the European (Geneva) office of the United Nations. Its budget is a part of the budget for that office. For library policy it looks to the director of the United Nations Library in New York for guidance.

CO-OPERATION WITH OTHER LIBRARIES

Great demands for interlibrary loans and other bibliographical services are made by the United Nations Library on other libraries. From a contractual fund in its budget the Library is able to pay for some of the services rendered by the Library of Congress and the New York Public Library, on which the demands are excessive. But they, like other libraries, also willingly provide many services without thought of remuneration.

THE USE OF EXPERTS

Mr. Verner Clapp, in a recent survey of the United Nations Library, says that it "is undoubtedly the most 'surveyed' library in the world" and lists twenty studies by outside experts of special problems. Many of the policies and procedures adopted from 1947 to date (some of which have been mentioned in this article) have resulted from the recommendations of these surveyors. *

---

*In the preparation of this article I have drawn on the acting director's recent reports. From him and other members of the staff I have also had much personal assistance. The opinions expressed are the author's.

INDEX OF PERSONAL NAMES
IN DIARY